THE
DISCIPLESHIP
DIFFERENCE

MAKING DISCIPLES WHILE
GROWING AS DISCIPLES

by Robert E. Logan and Charles R. Ridley

THE DISCIPLESHIP DIFFERENCE
MAKING DISCIPLES WHILE GROWING AS DISCIPLES
by Robert E. Logan and Charles R. Ridley

by Logan Leadership

44955-00-3
1-944955-00-7

SA
n

18 17 16 15   10 9 8 7 6 5 4 3 2 1

CHARLES R. RIDLEY

Acknowledgements

Thank you to all of those colleagues in ministry who gave us feedback on early manuscripts: **Colin Noyes, Kendra Diehl, Mark McGeever, Tom Greener, John Jackson, Jeff Norris, Mark Fields, Steve Fitch, Wayne Krause, Dave DeVries, and Luke Geraty.** Your perspectives helped us fill gaps, answer questions, and clarify salient points.

A big thanks to **Jennifer Dopazo**, whose formatting of this book has made it so much more reader-friendly, and to **Julia Michaud**, whose illustrations illuminate its concepts. Thanks to **Carl Simmons** for a fantastic editing job—your careful eye is much needed and appreciated. And thanks to **Tara Miller**, whose writing skills took the ideas generated in many hours of Skype calls with us and distilled them into a clearly written form.

We are as always grateful to our spouses, **Janet Logan** and **Mary Shaw-Ridley**, for their time, encouragement and ceaseless support.

And of course, our great gratitude goes out to all the people we've discipled through the years and all the people who have discipled us. This book would not have been possible without all we've learned from you about the ways God works toward maturing his people in our various paths of discipleship.

CONTENTS

CHAPTER I

WHERE'S THE TRANSFORMATION?

"Why am I even bothering to do this?" Rob thought to himself as he stacked the chairs. The sky outside the window was darkening, and he could hear the last of the cars pulling out of the church parking lot.

Rob has been the pastor at First Community Church for almost nine years now, ever since he finished seminary. He knew that the other students who had graduated with him considered him lucky. To get a lead pastor position with his denomination right after graduation... almost no one gets that. And it wasn't even in a bad location. This was a mid-sized town with decent schools. Definitely a plum position.

Yet Rob wasn't feeling particularly grateful right now. He had learned a great deal about leadership over the years—all the things that they didn't teach in seminary and which were now a part of *daily life when actually leading a church: listening well, getting people on board with new initiatives, refereeing conflicts and crises.*

Under his watch, the congregation had grown from one hundred to two hundred. Not stellar growth, maybe, but certainly not bad compared with some other churches in the area. He knew of two churches that had actually gone under recently. In fact, when he was willing to be honest, he had to admit that some of his congregation's growth had come from people leaving those churches.

But now in his late thirties, Rob felt trapped and frustrated, particularly in regard to his recent discipleship initiatives. He'd been teaching classes on discipleship for several months now, but clearly his current approach wasn't working. Rob had envisioned something life-changing and transformative... people excited about their relationship with God and living out their faith in fresh new ways. He was thinking of discipleship being lived out the way it had been in the New Testament... following Jesus at great cost and with great enthusiasm. Standing apart and being different. The city on a hill.

Instead, people were treating his discipleship class like... well, like a class. They'd chime in with the right answers when he asked questions. They did most of the assigned reading beforehand. Then after class they'd say things like, "Great teaching today, Pastor Rob," "Very educational. Some of that was new material for me," and "Thanks for the edification and encouragement." Comments like those left Rob cold... and asking one crucial question: Where's the transformation?

Rob found himself carrying on a one-sided conversation in his head as he cleaned up the classroom: "I'm getting people through these classes, but nothing really comes of it. They are more knowledgeable, maybe, but that knowledge doesn't seem to be making any real-world difference. It's not changing their lives. This is supposed to be discipleship. I might be seeing more educated disciples, but I'm not seeing better disciples. And I'm certainly not seeing more disciples. Where's the transformation?"

At that, Rob clicked out the lights and went home.

He may have been feeling discouraged, but Rob was asking precisely the right question: Where's the transformation? If we want to make disciples, that's where we need to be looking for the evidence: transformation. And like so many of us in ministry, Rob isn't seeing it.

We invest a lot of time, thought and energy into our discipleship efforts. We teach classes, gather resource materials, design curriculum, arrange discipleship relationships. . . but at the end of the day, what change are we really seeing? How come we aren't seeing the kind of real-life results we're looking for? Why isn't it working? Where's the transformation?

What is discipleship all about? We are to love God, love others, and make disciples. That's the Great Commandment and the Great Commission put together. . . not bad shorthand for the life of faith. The first two—love God and love others— are the way we are to live our lives. The third one—make disciples—is the mission: to help others follow Jesus just as we are following Jesus.

Our making of disciples flows out of our life with God, to be certain. Yet in some ways, the order needs to be inverted as well: Only as we make disciples *are* we perfected in the faith. As we reach out, we are shaped and transformed. As we go about life, the mission of Jesus is to recognize the people in our sphere of influence and help them take the next steps toward God. Engaging in that mission results in not only an increased quality of relationships, but a changed life for us as well.

> *Yet in some ways, the order needs to be inverted as well: Only as we make disciples are we perfected in the faith. As we reach out, we are shaped and transformed.*

We need to put the mission back at the center of our life of discipleship. Too often we have negated the mandate of Jesus. We have all the programs, but we're not focused on doing what Jesus called us to do right before he ascended. In our journey of discipleship, we need to become more engaged in making disciples.

Jesus said, "If you love me, keep my commands" (John 14:15). Our loving obedience will result in the transformation of our character—which, in turn, will lead to increased focus on the priority issues God has set before us. It's a cycle in which all the pieces are essential.

The purpose of this book is to unpack a different perspective than the one that guided Rob's discipleship class—and to instead reveal a perspective that results in transformation. *The Discipleship Difference* is different in three primary ways:

> **A different approach:** We treat different people differently, individualizing our approach to fit the uniqueness of each person.
>
> **A different process:** We make disciples at the same time as we are growing as disciples, not one first then the other.
>
> **A different outcome:** We move toward a holistic discipleship that includes loving God, loving others, and making disciples.

These three important differences are, in fact, *why* we named this book *The Discipleship Difference.* Consider how most discipleship programs work. If they have one at all, most churches offer some configuration of classes, readings, activities, and one-on-one meetings that serve as a "curriculum." When you finish those items, usually within six months to a year, you have finished the discipleship program. You are now qualified, if you choose, to be a discipler or a disciplemaker. You can then work with other people to help them along this same program.

This kind of assembly-line disciplemaking—which often results in no activity outside the classroom anyway—isn't even close to how Jesus approached making disciples. What we're talking about in *The Discipleship Difference* is a new—and yet very old—way of making disciples. It aligns with how Jesus made disciples.

A DIFFERENT APPROACH

Every person is different and we all reflect God in different ways. So why is our typical approach to discipleship the same across the board?

In the approach we'll be laying out here, disciplemakers help shape the environments, the relationships, and the processes in a way that maximizes people's unique path of growth as they take increasing responsibility for their own development. It's not just a classroom—and it's customized.

Let's start by considering the first meetings Jesus had with various people. Upon initially meeting people, how did he engage with them?

To Peter and Andrew, Jesus called them to follow him:
As Jesus was walking beside the Sea of Galilee, he saw two brothers, Simon called Peter and his brother Andrew. They were casting a net into the lake, for they were fishermen. "Come, follow me," Jesus said, "and I will send you out to fish for people." At once they left their nets and followed him (Matthew 4:18-20).

To a demon-possessed man he had healed, Jesus denied a request to go along with him:
As Jesus was getting into the boat, the man who had been demon-possessed begged to go with him. Jesus did not let him, but said, "Go home to your own people and tell them how much the Lord has done for you, and how he has had mercy on you." So the man went away and began to tell in the Decapolis how much Jesus had done for him. And all the people were amazed (Mark 5:18-20).

To Nathanael, Jesus told him about his own good character:
When Jesus saw Nathanael approaching, he said of him, "Here truly is an Israelite in whom there is no deceit." "How do you know me?" Nathanael asked. Jesus answered, "I saw you while you were still under the fig tree before Philip called you." Then

Nathanael declared, "Rabbi, you are the Son of God; you are the king of Israel" (John 1:47–49).

To the woman at the well, Jesus offered her living water and told of her history of sin:
When a Samaritan woman came to draw water, Jesus said to her, "Will you give me a drink?" (His disciples had gone into the town to buy food.) The Samaritan woman said to him, "You are a Jew and I am a Samaritan woman. How can you ask me for a drink?" (For Jews do not associate with Samaritans.) Jesus answered her, "If you knew the gift of God and who it is that asks you for a drink, you would have asked him and he would have given you living water. . . He told her, "Go, call your husband and come back." "I have no husband," she replied. Jesus said to her, "You are right when you say you have no husband. The fact is, you have had five husbands, and the man you now have is not your husband. What you have just said is quite true" (John 4:7–10, 16–18).

To the self-righteous, Jesus told a story comparing them unfavorably to robbers, evildoers, and adulterers:
To some who were confident of their own righteousness and looked down on everyone else, Jesus told this parable: "Two men went up to the temple to pray, one a Pharisee and the other a tax collector. The Pharisee stood by himself and prayed: 'God, I thank you that I am not like other people—robbers, evildoers, adulterers—or even like this tax collector. I fast twice a week and give a tenth of all I get.' "But the tax collector stood at a distance. He would not even look up to heaven, but beat his breast and said, 'God, have mercy on me, a sinner.' "I tell you that this man, rather than the other, went home justified before God. For all those who exalt themselves will be humbled, and those who humble themselves will be exalted" (Luke 18:9–14).

To Zacchaeus, the wealthy tax collector, Jesus invited himself over for dinner:
Jesus entered Jericho and was passing through. A man was there by the name of Zacchaeus; he was a chief tax collector and was wealthy. He wanted to see who Jesus was, but

because he was short he could not see over the crowd. So he ran ahead and climbed a sycamore-fig tree to see him, since Jesus was coming that way. When Jesus reached the spot, he looked up and said to him, "Zacchaeus, come down immediately. I must stay at your house today." So he came down at once and welcomed him gladly (Luke 19:1–6).

To a rich man who asked Jesus what he should do, Jesus told him to give away all his possessions:
Jesus answered, "If you want to be perfect, go, sell your possessions and give to the poor, and you will have treasure in heaven. Then come, follow me." When the young man heard this, he went away sad, because he had great wealth (Matthew 19:21–22).

To the Pharisee Nicodemus, Jesus took a philosophical approach:
Now there was a Pharisee, a man named Nicodemus who was a member of the Jewish ruling council. He came to Jesus at night and said, "Rabbi, we know that you are a teacher who has come from God. For no one could perform the signs you are doing if God were not with him." Jesus replied, "Very truly I tell you, no one can see the kingdom of God unless they are born again." "How can someone be born when they are old?" Nicodemus asked. "Surely they cannot enter a second time into their mother's womb to be born!" Jesus answered, "Very truly I tell you, no one can enter the kingdom of God unless they are born of water and the Spirit. Flesh gives birth to flesh, but the Spirit gives birth to spirit. You should not be surprised at my saying, 'You must be born again.' The wind blows wherever it pleases. You hear its sound, but you cannot tell where it comes from or where it is going. So it is with everyone born of the Spirit." "How can this be?" Nicodemus asked (John 3:1–9).

To a Roman soldier, Jesus complimented his faith and granted his request for healing:
When Jesus had entered Capernaum, a centurion came to him, asking for help. "Lord," he said, "my servant lies at home paralyzed, suffering terribly." Jesus said to him, "Shall I come and

heal him?" The centurion replied, "Lord, I do not deserve to have you come under my roof. But just say the word, and my servant will be healed. For I myself am a man under authority, with soldiers under me. I tell this one, 'Go,' and he goes; and that one, 'Come,' and he comes. I say to my servant, 'Do this,' and he does it." When Jesus heard this, he was amazed and said to those following him, "Truly I tell you, I have not found anyone in Israel with such great faith" (Matthew 8:5-10).

The moral of these stories? Jesus had a common goal for everyone—but he approached every person differently. He didn't say the same thing to everyone, and he didn't recommend the same course of action to everyone. He took people where they were, treating them according to their history and according to what they needed in order to move forward. Some people needed a sharp challenge. Some people needed mercy and embrace. Some people needed to think and ponder from a new perspective. Some people needed to take dramatic action. Some people needed to spend time with Jesus. Some people needed to be sent out to engage others. Some people simply needed to be recognized and known.

> *The moral of these stories? Jesus had a common goal for everyone—but he approached every person differently.*

By listening to the Holy Spirit, we too can discern what each person needs. Effective discipleship responds to the differences among people. That responsiveness does not minimize their ultimate need for God and his expectations of them, but the way we approach making disciples must be suited to the uniqueness of each person. We are not all the same. We don't all have the same struggles. We don't all have the same life experiences. And we certainly don't all begin at identical starting points in our discipleship journey.

At different stages of our lives, we need to focus in different areas. And we all need different input, because we grow and develop differently. Do all of us need to read the same book, take the same class, or participate in the same activity? Probably not.

In short, rather than trying to fit people into our discipleship program, we should try to tailor our approach to discipleship so that it fits unique individuals. That's the discipleship difference.

A DIFFERENT PROCESS

Unlike an assembly line, we never come away with a completed product. No one ever "graduates" from discipleship. We make disciples at the same time we are growing as disciples. . . and we never finish. The cycle simultaneously involves being and making disciples, in a never-ending process of growth.

> *We make disciples at the same time we are growing as disciples. . . and we never finish.*

There is no reason for us to finish a course of study before telling others about Jesus. In fact, it's unbiblical. Remember the story of the demon-possessed man?

As Jesus was getting into the boat, the man who had been demon-possessed begged to go with him. Jesus did not let him, but said, "Go home to your own people and tell them how much the Lord has done for you, and how he has had mercy on you." So the man went away and began to tell in the Decapolis how much Jesus had done for him. And all the people were amazed (Mark 5:18–20).

We don't need to know everything. We simply need to bear witness to what we have experienced. Brand-new believers can often make a significant impact on their families and friends. As they experience the goodness of God, they can naturally start sharing that experience with people they know.

When we encourage new believers to become more and more engaged with Christians to the exclusion of others, however well-intentioned, we inadvertently remove them from their natural sphere of relationships. This posture is like being "not of the world" and "not in the world," instead of "in the world" but "not of the world." In taking it, we often do them—and their friends—a great disservice. We place a limitation on their growth as disciples and the potential growth of their families and friends.

The fact is: We need to be engaged in making disciples in order to continue growing. How can we expect to grow toward maturity if we are not obeying the commands of Jesus that we already know. . . like "make disciples"?

Following the pattern of Jesus, we are to go to where the people are—and that's outside the walls of the church. We are to meet them where they are, both geographically and spiritually. It doesn't matter if we're not finished products ourselves. That's okay—no one else expects us to be perfect. People just expect us to be honest about where we are right now.

Hopefully as we grow we'll become increasingly effective at making disciples. But that doesn't mean we shouldn't start now. Making disciples isn't optional, and no Christian should be sitting on the sidelines; it's part of what it means to be a disciple. Formation and multiplication together are what will truly make a difference for the kingdom.

A DIFFERENT OUTCOME

In addition to a difference in approach (treating people as unique individuals) and a difference in process (growing as disciples and making disciples at the same time), there is a third difference—a difference in outcome. What is the outcome of being a disciple? What are we aiming toward?

Jesus told us to love God, love others, and make disciples. Taken together, these result in a holistic approach to discipleship. It includes all of us: our vertical relationship with God, our horizontal relationships with one another, and our commitment to the disciple-making mission of Jesus.

If we start with making disciples, holistic discipleship follows. Discipleship is doing life with Jesus among other people. When we start walking alongside others honestly, we understand quickly where the holes are in our own lives. As we grow in each area, we become more fully integrated as followers of Jesus.

Many discipleship models emphasize one or two of these areas, to the exclusion of the other(s). A real disciple needs to embrace and be growing in all dimensions of discipleship. We can't be two-thirds of a disciple, picking and choosing our preferred areas for growth. True discipleship is holistic: We can't be content to be growing in some areas and lacking in other areas. A disciple, when fully trained, is like his or her teacher: Jesus (Luke 6:40).

We can't be two-thirds of a disciple, picking and choosing our preferred areas for growth.

It's about a healthy blend of loving God, loving others, and making disciples. . . a blend that actually becomes healthier in the mixing. Each of these emphases, by themselves, fails to achieve a holistic, robust discipleship. That's one of the reasons we aren't seeing the transformation we desire—because we need all three. We need the whole package.

The discipleship perspective described here allows us to listen to the leading of the Holy Spirit and be less controlling in our approach to what it means to disciple other people. If we trust the Spirit and trust that others can listen to him as well, we are freed to diverge from the beaten path of discipleship in a way that breaks new ground . . . a way that takes people where they are and helps them develop in the areas they need. This kind of holistic development results in both better disciples *and* more disciples.

It doesn't work to create non-disciple-making disciples. That's a contradiction in terms. The terms "disciplemaking" and "discipleship" should be synonymous. Disciplemaking is part of the very identity of a disciple. We make disciples as we live out our discipleship.

Ten Principles That Reflect How Jesus Made Disciples

Jesus' approach to discipleship centered on himself and on the gospel of grace. Radical grace fuels radical obedience in disciples. Our obedience cannot be founded on fear, guilt, selfish ambition, or trying to merit God's favor.

Given this foundation, we are to watch the Master, and then do as he did. After all, Jesus was called Rabbi, meaning teacher; likewise, we are to watch, imitate, and learn from him just as his original disciples did. Consider how Jesus went about making disciples. What observations can we make?

Principle #1: Jesus made disciples of ordinary people, not superstars. His disciples were fishermen, not rabbinical students. They were tax collectors and the poor, widows and prostitutes. The people who became followers of Jesus in the gospel accounts were comprised simply of the people who were at hand.

These were the people who were around and available.

Lesson for us: Discipleship is for everyone. It's not the fast track or the honors course- it's for ordinary people. . . everyone.

Principle #2: Jesus started with unbelievers, and made disciples outside of church. Jesus didn't do much recruiting within the temple. For example, he called fishermen who were minding their own business, focused on earning their living. They didn't have to already believe that Jesus was the Son of God or agree to a doctrinal statement; they just had to be willing to follow him and see.

Lesson for us: People don't have to be Christians to begin the journey of discipleship, just willing to explore.

Principle #3: Jesus expected that his disciples would make more disciples. First, Jesus sent out the twelve disciples:

> When Jesus had called the Twelve together, he gave them power and authority to drive out all demons and to cure diseases, and he sent them out to proclaim the kingdom of God and to heal the sick. . . So they set out and went from village to village, proclaiming the good news and healing people everywhere (Luke 9:1–2, 6).

Then in the very next chapter, we see Jesus sending out seventy-two disciples:

> After this the Lord appointed seventy-two others and sent them two by two ahead of him to every town and place where he was about to go. He told them, "The harvest is plentiful, but the workers are few. Ask the Lord of the harvest, therefore, to send out workers into his harvest field. Go! I am sending you out like lambs among wolves" (Luke 10:1–3).

Lesson for us: Being sent out to make more disciples is a given. It's what disciples *do*.

Principle #4: Jesus made disciples within the context of relationships. He went to parties, weddings, people's homes for dinner. People introduced him to their friends. In this way, Jesus became involved in natural networks of relationships: "While Jesus was having dinner at Levi's house, many tax collectors and sinners were eating with him and his disciples, for there were many who followed him" (Mark 2:15).

Lesson for us: Pay attention to the people around you, in your natural network of relationships.

Principle #5: Jesus skewed discipleship toward the practical rather than the academic. Jesus did teach. And when we consider behavior and character, we recognize that there are certain knowledge-based elements for living that out. Jesus didn't neglect those. But he went beyond standard academic teaching, basing most of his discipleship on modeling and on spontaneous life situations that arose in the moment, as well as through the use of everyday illustrations people could understand. Consider casting out demons and the feeding of the five thousand as examples.

Lesson for us: Whenever you have a choice between hands-on learning and classroom learning, go with hands-on learning. It sticks better anyway.

Principle #6: Jesus took people where they were at and started there. Seven husbands, demon-possession, Pharisee, natural skeptic—wherever you were, Jesus would meet you there. He invited everyone into relationship on a foundation of love and grace. Although there are certainly actions and behaviors involved, discipleship is first and foremost a grace-based relationship with Jesus.

Lesson for us: Never count anyone out as a potential disciple. Remember that "whosoever will" may come, as an invitation of the gospel of grace.

Principle #7: Jesus dealt with people differently at different times of their lives. Consider how Jesus engaged with the twelve disciples. Sometimes he was patient with them and explained things. Sometimes he rebuked them. Sometimes he asked them to reflect on what they were doing. Sometimes he answered their questions and sometimes he refused.

Lesson for us: Be flexible. Even the same person needs different input and types of feedback at different times in their lives of discipleship.

Principle #8: Jesus recognized and accepted that discipleship is a process, complete with setbacks. After three years of following Jesus, Peter denied that he even knew Jesus. Jesus had been arrested and Peter was afraid. But Jesus knew that wasn't the end of the story.

Lesson for us: Everybody has weaknesses and everybody fails sometimes. That doesn't mean they're not disciples.

Principle #9: Jesus assumed discipleship to be holistic in nature, touching on and transforming all areas of life. That means our relationships, our money, our calling and purpose, our intimacy with God . . . everything. "Anyone who loves their father or mother more than me is not worthy of me; anyone who loves their son or daughter more than me is not worthy of me. Whoever does not take up their cross and follow me is not worthy of me. Whoever finds their life will lose it, and whoever loses their life for my sake will find it" (Matthew 10:37–39).

Lesson for us: Discipleship will impact every area of a person's life—not just the "spiritual" parts.

Principle #10: Jesus intended for disciplemaking to continue through the generations, multiplying across cultures. Jesus' approach to disciplemaking resulted in a multiplication of communities of Jesus followers. There were twelve disciples, then seventy-two, then 120 at the time of Jesus' resurrection. By Pentecost, there were three thousand. When Jesus gave the

Great Commission to make disciples of all nations, he expected his disciples to follow his pattern. "But you will receive power when the Holy Spirit comes on you; and you will be my witnesses in Jerusalem, and in all Judea and Samaria, *and to the ends of the earth*" (Acts 1:8, emphasis added).

Lesson for us: Disciplemaking is what Jesus wants us to focus on until his return, without any regard to geography, race, language, culture, or generation.

Taken together with what we saw earlier about how Jesus treated different people differently, what do we see here? It's kind of messy, to be honest. People are going in all different directions, focusing in different areas, growing themselves at the same time they're helping others to grow. They're dealing with their inner lives at the same time as they're dealing with their outward service. Sometimes it's one step forward, two steps back, and they're figuring it out as they go.

Basically, if you're the kind of person who wants to diagram all of this into a chart, you're in for a really big challenge.

Jesus' discipleship was not linear and was not one-size-fits-all, and it's not easy. But if you want to guide others along their spiritual journeys in a way that respects their differences, allows the Holy Spirit to lead, and results in the multiplication of disciples and disciplemakers, this book was written with you in mind.

You can go off-script, while never going off Scripture.

You can go off-script, while never going off Scripture. Jesus modeled that for us. He did not follow the formal prescription touted by the religious establishment of his day. Instead, he met people where they were and treated them as individuals.

He encouraged them to tell others about him and to make disciples right from the very beginning. He shared a vision of discipleship that was holistic and integrated, not separating mind, body, and spirit. That may be a little messier and less linear than what we're used to, but it's a whole lot more faithful to what Jesus modeled for us. And our engagement in the mission of Jesus—to make disciples—will be the engine that drives everything else.

With the Great Commission, Jesus called us to make disciples of all peoples. As a skilled carpenter, Jesus understood how to take wood in raw and unfinished form and craft it into useful products, starting with whatever wood was there. And like the carpenter's apprenticeship process, the discipleship process isn't just about making disciples, but training those disciples to make more disciples—passing along the knowledge, skills, and passion necessary for the work.

This is the responsibility of all believers: to be and to make disciples. In the following pages, *The Discipleship Difference* lays out an intentional, holistic, and relational approach to discipleship that is individualized to meet each person wherever they are.

THE WAY FORWARD

In this book, we will first take a closer look at what a disciple is and does. After all, we need to know where we're going in order to have any real hope of getting there. We'll then explore the roots of the discipleship journey—in the harvest, not at conversion—addressing one common and damaging misconception in particular. We'll also provide some guidance for self-assessment (discovering our individual starting points), as well as how to hear God's voice and move forward from there. After that, we'll explore strategies for developing disciples in the context of reproducible groups, maintaining an outward focus, and the important dynamics of focused discipling relationships for individuals. Finally, we'll unpack specific discipleship skills and how we can support one another on this journey together as we carry out the Great Commission.

In the back of the book, you'll find questions for reflection, discussion, or team processing. There are questions for each chapter, but we have put all of them in the back so as to not break the flow of the story.

Throughout this book, you'll also see the journey of Pastor Rob (whom you met at the beginning of this chapter) unfold. The content within the chapters will then help you unpack the practical insights you can use in your own ministry.

It doesn't matter who you are or what your role is. If you're a follower of Jesus, all of this applies to you. You could be a volunteer leader, a pastor like Rob, a coach, or a denominational leader. You may be young or old, new in the faith or a believer for many years. Regardless of your official role, if you're reading this book, you're probably someone who wants to see something different on the horizon. You're someone who wants to see real discipleship and the transformation it brings, to ourselves and to the world around us.

We encourage you to follow along on Pastor Rob's journey and put the principles into practice in your own journey. When we approach discipleship holistically, in the way Jesus modeled for us, we get the transformation we are looking for. We begin living as the hands, feet, and voice of Jesus in the world today; and as we do, we make a difference.

Where's the transformation? That's precisely the right question. Let's find out.

CHAPTER 2

WHAT DOES A DISCIPLE LOOK LIKE?

The following week, Rob was sitting in a coffee shop in town, journaling some of his thoughts. He'd been journaling since the discipleship class last week, but the writing seemed to be just going in circles. He wasn't getting any closer to a solution—or even any insight.

"Pastor Blaine?" Rob looked up to see a man in his seventies who looked vaguely familiar. "I thought that was you. I'm Jim Tucker. Caught your sermon this weekend, as I'm in town visiting my daughter and her family."

"Oh! You're Lisa's dad. I thought you looked familiar but I couldn't quite place you. She told me you're in town for the next few months from the mission field. You're serving in Honduras?"

"Was serving in Honduras, and India before that. But I'm retired now. So I came to town to see grandkids and figure out what God has for me next."

"Well, not much going on here, unfortunately. Probably nothing compared to what you're used to seeing on the mission field. I was just conducting a post-mortem on my latest discipleship class," said Rob, gesturing to his journal.

"That bad?" Jim raised his eyebrows. "I bet I've had worse. Sometimes it takes a lot of wrong turns before you can find your way."

"Any advice for me?"

"How long do you have?" Jim laughed. "Us old guys can get talking and it's hard to shut us up, you know."

"Have a seat," smiled Rob, indicating the empty chair across from him.

Jim asked what he'd tried so far, and Rob explained what he'd been doing with the discipleship classes, including all the time and the planning. "But they just aren't working," he finished. "I'm not getting the results I was hoping for."

"What results were you hoping for?" asked Jim.

That question pulled Rob up short. He had to pause for a minute to think about it, and even then he wasn't sure he'd be able to articulate a good answer. "Well, not this. More action, I guess. More life transformation. I guess I figured I'd know it when I saw it."

They sat in silence for a while, as Rob absorbed the fact that he didn't know exactly what he had even been aiming for... No wonder I hadn't hit it, he thought with dismay. Then he looked over at Jim. "What does a disciple even look like, anyway? What does he or she actually do?" Rob paused, considering. "I think I've been gearing my classes more toward what a disciple should know instead of what they should do."

"Sounds to me like you have an assignment for the week," observed Jim. "I know of one church that started with just the Great Commandment and the Great Commission: love God, love others, make disciples. From there, they tried to figure out all the behaviors a disciple would need to do in order to live out those three commands. Why don't you try reading through the Gospels and see what kinds of behaviors you see disciples engaging in?"

"That may take more than a week."

"True," Jim shrugged, "but you need to start somewhere. Want to meet up next week and see what you've got so far?"

"Absolutely. Same time, same place?"

In order to grow into mature disciples, we need to know what we're aiming for. Stephen Covey was on point when he said, "Begin with the end in mind." Instead of just moving toward some kind of vague sense of "maturity," we should spend some time thinking through what a fully formed disciple of Jesus looks like. What qualities and behaviors would indicate that someone is following Jesus?

So what standards are we measuring ourselves by? Only when we've seen that picture are we able to move intentionally toward it. Just as an archer must know what the target looks like and where it is in order to hit it accurately, we need some external reference for what a disciple looks like. We need to know clearly what we are aiming for in our discipleship, in order to have any real chance of hitting the target.

What qualities and behaviors are we trying to develop in disciples? What do we want them to do? What do we want them to be? Unfortunately, many Christians can only vaguely answer these questions. We need to know what a disciple looks like before we can be intentional about growing as disciples ourselves, and before we can make disciples of others.

We need to know what a disciple looks like before we can be intentional about growing as disciples ourselves, and before we can make disciples of others.

Without a clear picture, we are left to guess. None of us are perfect; we each have our shortcomings and blind spots. As we live our own life of discipleship—and as we disciple others—we tend to focus on our strengths and avoid areas where we are weak. We need an objective picture of what a disciple looks like in order to avoid simply projecting our own preferences.

Having an objective picture doesn't mean putting everyone in the same box. The way discipleship looks on one person is different than the way it looks on another. We are all individuals, created by God to be unique. Yet, as we examine the concept of discipleship in Scripture, we find that God has called all of us to certain central elements. For example, hospitality may look different for Bob than it does for Chuck, but we are all called to live hospitality out in some form.

Making Sure the Target Is Measurable and Behavioral

So what specific qualities are we looking for? We have found that a focus on behavior rather than knowledge yields a clearer picture of a disciple, even when the expression of specific discipleship behaviors may vary from person to person.

Discipleship is not only about knowledge (2 Peter 3:18); it's about character, behavior, attitudes, a posture of humility, teachability—and grace for continued growth. Knowledge may be a building block, but it's not enough on its own. By itself, knowledge puffs up. The heart of discipleship displays Jesus to those around us in a way that they can see. If there's something real on the inside, it needs to be observable on the outside. Inner qualities can only be seen through behaviors.

If Jesus commanded us to make disciples—and he did—we should have some clarity on what we are trying to produce. How would we know a disciple if we saw one? How do we know if we or others are moving in the right direction? There should be visible expressions of discipleship that can be observed by those around us.

Behaviors can be measured through words and deeds. It's about how we live. So what we need to measure is not how many minutes you read the Bible per day, but the degree to which you live out the principles of the Word of God in your life. As Christ the incarnate Word of God became flesh, so should our knowledge of the Word of God be translated—incarnated—into human action.

That's an important distinction. Some people might spend a great deal of time reading Scripture, yet aren't allowing it to impact their lives in a transformative way. They aren't applying it. Although it would be easier to measure minutes, what we need to look at as we measure discipleship are behavioral expressions that are a reflection of general life change. We're looking at the fruit, not the specific method of getting the fruit.

IF YOU CARE ABOUT THE RESEARCH...
A NOTE FROM CHUCK

Setting hard goals—those that are specific and high—results in better outcomes than goals that are easy or vague.[2] In addition, meeting three criteria improves the likelihood of achieving those goals: personal commitment to the goals, ability to attain the goals, and the absence of conflicting goals. Furthermore, goal-setting is a "discrepancy-creating process." People who seek to attain new goals are discontent with their present condition and want a more desirable outcome. This research implies that a specific portrait of what it means to be a disciple is a more valuable resource than the all-too-common and undefined exhortation of discipleship. Without a clear picture, we can anticipate nominal commitment to discipleship, an inexact measurement of one's strengths and weaknesses as a disciple, and the uncertainty of conflicting goals to disciple formation. Finally, we will have no basis for determining if there is a discrepancy between where a person begins in the discipleship journey and the markers of development as a disciple.

The Tree of Discipleship

As we've considered the nature of discipleship, we've created a diagram to represent the eight dimensions of a disciple. This "tree of discipleship" is one way to define what a disciple is and does, so that we can move toward that target.

Our essential starting point was the portrait of Jesus provided by the four gospel accounts. Using this picture as our guide, we began by looking at the specific reported behaviors of Jesus. From there, we put together a composite picture that holistically reflects those components. As Jesus became incarnate and lived among us, these are the ways we see him living.

The resulting tree of discipleship is a much clearer picture of what it means to live and love like Jesus. Take a look at the diagram and categories that follow, and then evaluate your own life. Allow others to speak into your life as well. We never travel alone on the journey of allowing God to work in our lives.

Experiencing God:
Intentionally and consistently engaging with God in such a way that you open yourself to a deeper understanding of him and deeper relationship with him

Supporting Scriptures:
> He answered, "Love the Lord your God with all your heart and with all your soul and with all your strength and with all your mind" and, "Love your neighbor as yourself" (Luke 10:27).

Behavioral Expressions:
- Increasing your awareness of God's love and presence
- Growing in the knowledge and grace of God
- Reflecting on and applying Scripture in your everyday life
- Dialoguing authentically with God
- Worshipping God in spirit and in truth

Spiritual Responsiveness:
Actively listening to the Holy Spirit and taking action according to what you are hearing

Supporting Scriptures:
> Since we are living by the Spirit, let us follow the Spirit's leading in every part of our lives (Galatians 5:25, NLT). Trust in the Lord with all your heart; do not depend on your own understanding. Seek his will in all you do, and he will show you which path to take (Proverbs 3:5-6, NLT).
> Do not merely listen to the word, and so deceive yourselves. Do what it says (James 1:22).

Behavioral Expressions:
- Receiving guidance and empowerment from the Holy Spirit
- Discerning opportunities for involvement in God's work
- Checking what you're hearing with Scripture, and with your faith community
- Acting in faith through loving obedience
- Listening for God's calling in your life

Sacrificial Service:
Doing good works even when it's costly, inconvenient, or challenging

Supporting Scriptures
For we are God's masterpiece. He has created us anew in Christ Jesus, so we can do the good things he planned for us long ago (Ephesians 2:10, NLT).
Their only suggestion was that we keep on helping the poor, which I have always been eager to do (Galatians 2:10, NLT).

Behavioral Expression.
- Blessing others with your words and deeds
- Partnering with others to minister in practical ways
- Ministering personally and appropriately to the poor
- Speaking up for people experiencing injustice
- Cultivating a compassionate heart

Generous Living:
Faithfully stewarding what God has given you, so that you can contribute toward the advancement of the kingdom

Supporting Scriptures
Again, the Kingdom of Heaven can be illustrated by the story of a man going on a long trip. He called together his servants and entrusted his money to them while he was gone. He gave five bags of silver to one, two bags of silver to another, and one bag of silver to the last—dividing it in proportion to their abilities. He then left on his trip (Matthew 25:14–15, NLT).
If you are faithful in little things, you will be faithful in large ones. But if you are dishonest in little things, you won't be honest with greater responsibilities (Luke 16:10, NLT).

Behavioral Expressions:
- Managing your time and resources for kingdom purposes
- Using your spiritual gifts to bless others
- Giving your money generously and wisely
- Showing hospitality without favoritism
- Living out your God-given calling

Disciplemaking:
Living in obedience to the Great Commission given by Jesus, which entails making more and better followers of Christ

Supporting Scripture:
> Therefore, go and make disciples of all the nations, baptizing them in the name of the Father and the Son and the Holy Spirit. Teach these new disciples to obey all the commands I have given you. And be sure of this: I am with you always, even to the end of the age (Matthew 28:19–20, NLT).

Behavioral Expressions:
- Engaging in spiritual conversations with those who are not yet followers of Jesus
- Explaining the good news and the way of Jesus
- Establishing new believers in a discipleship process
- Connecting people with a faith community
- Helping new followers make more followers

Personal Transformation:
Changing your attitudes and behaviors in positive ways, as a result of your relationship with God and others

Supporting Scripture:
> Don't copy the behavior and customs of this world, but let God transform you into a new person by changing the way you think. Then you will learn to know God's will for you, which is good and pleasing and perfect (Romans 12:2, NLT).

Behavioral Expression
- Actively engaging with God in the examination of your heart
- Cooperating with God's healing work in your life
- Processing feedback and input from others
- Living out new priorities and changed behavior
- Increasingly bearing the fruit of the Spirit

Authentic Relationships:
Engaging with other people in ways that reflect the heart of God toward them

Supporting Scripture:
Do to others whatever you would like them to do to you. This is the essence of all that is taught in the law and the prophets (Matthew 7:12).

Behavioral Expression
- Showing respect for all people
- Forgiving others and asking forgiveness
- Confronting others with humility as necessary
- Praying with and for others
- Supporting each other honestly through life challenges

Community Transformation:
Personal involvement with others to facilitate positive change where you live—and beyond

Supporting Scriptures
And the one sitting on the throne said, "Look, I am making everything new!" (Revelation 21:5a, NLT).
Now all glory to God, who is able, through his mighty power at work within us, to accomplish infinitely more than we might ask or think. Glory to him in the church and in Christ Jesus through all generations forever and ever! Amen (Ephesians 3:20-21).

Behavioral Expressions:
- Participating in a faith community that reaches outside of itself
- Praying for healing and reconciliation in society
- Involving yourself in social justice needs in the broader community
- Caring for God's creation in practical ways
- Helping others cultivate healthy lives and relationships

Reflecting on the Tree of Discipleship

Although different groups may tailor their language to fit their ethos and values, the tree of discipleship provides a remarkably inclusive picture of our identity as a people of God.

As you look at the diagram of the tree, you'll notice a progression of becoming increasingly more like Jesus. We are rooted in God, and our behaviors flow out of our response to his presence: serving, living generously, helping others become followers of Jesus. As we engage with God and others in this way, we are transformed, able to form authentic relationships, and participate in the broader transformation that God is bringing about.

As we put together a composite picture that holistically reflects these eight qualities of a disciple, we see inevitable interconnectedness and overlap. Generous living blends into sacrificial service at points. Personal transformation is necessary for authentic relationships. Disciplemaking, at the very top of the tree, is the outcome of being a disciple, but it is not possible without the roots, trunk, and rest of the branches. We can't pull apart and isolate the eight qualities from one another. They are like the petals of a flower—distinct but overlapping.

Now, this tree of discipleship is only one way of defining discipleship and trying to break it down into its component parts. There are certainly other ways of looking at it as well. So we challenge you: Delve into it. What's missing? What's *not* needed? Tear it apart nd rebuild it until you're satisfied with it. Cross-check it against the fruit of the Spirit, the Beatitudes, the life of Jesus. . . any ot er cross-checks you can think of. Consider your own lif as well; don't allow this exercise to be just academic. In wha important ways has God grown and matured you? How dc these elements of discipleship play out in your life?

Ultimately, you need t. have a picture that you feel accurately reflects what a discipl is and does. Only then will you have clarity on what you're rying to produce in your own discipleship efforts.

Don't Wait for Perfec on

The tree of disciplesh is certainly not a perfect picture, but it does provide the m st holistic profile of discipleship we're aware of. If any of us ere able to live out even eighty percent of what's there, imagi e the impact the church would have.

Also, consider this qu stion: If you don't do this, what are you doing? What other or ions do you have? What tools or processes do you have in place to comprehensively develop your people as disciples? V hatever you do, do something. Do it biblically and do it int ntionally. Don't wait for perfection. Get something that's a go d starting point and refine it as you go. The key is to get start d.

Do not think of yourse f more highly than you ought, but rather think of yourself with ober judgment, in accordance with the faith God has distribu d to each of you (Romans 12:3).

IF YOU CARE ABOUT THE RESEARCH...
A NOTE FROM CHUCK

Transformation as a disciple is not the same as perfectionism. To use the Latin phrase *errare humanum*, "to err is human." As such, going through life without flaws is an impossibility. When Jesus said, "Be perfect," he was contrasting his expectation to the legalistic piety demonstrated by the scribes and Pharisees (Matthew 5:48). From a theological perspective, perfectionists do not embrace the freedom for which Christ has set us free (Galatians 5:1). From a psychological perspective, perfectionists are characterized by a number of negative traits: rigid dichotomous thinking, unrealistic goals, lowered self-esteem, and a destructive cycle.[3]

The following week, Rob came back to the coffee shop with an early-version drawing of the tree of discipleship. He had decided that experiencing and responding to God formed the roots and the trunk: the beneath-the-surface functions the tree needs in order to grow and produce fruit. The branches, then, were the more visible, behavioral results.

Jim pressed Rob on several points, insisting that he make sure the diagram was holistic. Rob brought the draft of his diagram to a few key people in his church to get feedback and to pray over it. Together, they decided to add the branch on sacrificial service and the end result of community transformation.

Rob was also concerned about not losing the knowledge aspect of discipleship. "After all, I'm a seminary-trained guy. I think understanding biblical principles is important to our character formation as disciples."

"Of course you do," agreed Jim. "So do I. I just think it's important to put knowledge in the most strategically helpful place. Let me ask you this: When have you done your best research into theological questions?"

Rob thought for a minute. "When I had an important question."

"Exactly," said Jim. "Knowledge supports the rest of life. What we learn must be connected to how we are living, to questions we run across, to problems we face. When we have a need is when we are most truly motivated to learn. Knowledge must be integrated into our character and relationships and actions. Right living requires an intake of Scripture and the renewing of our minds."

"So you're saying that the most strategic place for knowledge is digging deeper when we run across questions that affect our daily living."

"Precisely. In fact, I'm going to give you a theology assignment right now. I want you to refine this diagram you've created by adding some specific behaviors—subpoints, if you will—to each part of the tree. These behaviors will answer the question of what a disciple actually looks like in daily life."

Rob again revisited the Scripture, and spent time praying and thinking about the kinds of actions that indicate someone is truly following Jesus. After some refinement and feedback from the key people in his congregation, Rob looked at his tree of discipleship diagram and stepped back. Finally, he felt he had a clear sense of what a disciple looks like—not just in knowledge, but in deeds. This is what his discipleship efforts should be aiming for.

CHAPTER 3

DISCIPLESHIP STARTS IN THE HARVEST

Rob and Jim had settled into a weekly get-together at the coffee shop on Tuesday mornings. This Tuesday, Rob came in with a gust of wind traveling in behind him. Leaves swirled outside the glass door on the sidewalk.

Proudly, he placed his finished copy of the tree of discipleship diagram onto the table in front of Jim. After more than a month of work, trying to make sure it included all the important aspects of discipleship, praying and gathering input from others, Rob felt this version was truly final.

Jim studied it for a while. "Fabulous. Just fabulous. This looks great, Rob. Lattes on me this morning!"

After they settled in with their drinks, Rob spoke excitedly about the possibilities this clear picture of discipleship would open up for him: "Now that I know what I'm trying to develop, I can start to design some better way to get people there." He began thinking out loud: "Given that categories like sacrificial service and making new disciples are part of the discipleship tree, I'm thinking maybe a class isn't the best approach. That what we need isn't just theological education but maybe more engagement in the harvest?"

"Well, engagement in the harvest is certainly the place to start making disciples. After all, that's what Jesus did. He didn't go to the temple to look for disciples—he went to the seashore and the marketplaces, the wells, and the roads." Jim stopped and looked at Rob, "What are you personally doing to have relationships with people who don't know Jesus?"

"Me?" A few minutes of silence. "Ouch. Not a whole lot, to be completely honest. I guess I've been so focused on trying to get the people in my church to be disciples that I haven't been looking to the harvest myself. In fact, as a pastor, I spend virtually all my time with Christians. Not necessarily disciples, but Christians."

"What do you see as the difference. . . now that you've created this tree of discipleship?" asked Jim.

"'Christians'—the way many people currently use the term, not its actual meaning—means people who say they believe in Jesus and attend church. Disciples—followers of Jesus—are people whose actions indicate they are trying to live out what Jesus commanded them to do. Belief vs. behavior maybe, although of course I know those two aren't supposed to be separated. Am I making sense here? I don't want to sound heretical."

"I understand what you're saying, Rob. I've actually seen a lot of this in my ministry, both here and abroad. I've had people in my

churches who aren't really following Jesus. I used to call that phenomenon 'non-following believers.' After a lot of hitting my head against a brick wall—which I hope to save you the trouble of doing by telling you this—I discovered that I couldn't make them think their way into a new way of acting. Instead, they had to act their way into a new way of thinking. I also discovered that discipleship needed to start in the harvest fields, not in the church pews. And since I was the leader, it needed to start with me."

Rob leaned back in his chair. "We're talking about more than redesigning my church's discipleship program, aren't we?"

"Yes, we're talking about some major, and very important, paradigm shifts. Without making these shifts, you're not going to get much further than you have already... no matter what kind of program you use." Jim looked Rob in the eye. "I'm giving you another assignment, Rob. This week I want you to meditate on Philemon 1:6 (NIV 84): 'I pray that you may be active in sharing your faith, so that you will have a full understanding of every good thing we have in Christ.' Now, as you might remember from your seminary Greek class, koinonia means not only fellowship but also sharing. I want you to spend some time thinking about how your own personal engagement with people who don't know Jesus is essential to your own spiritual growth."

IF YOU CARE ABOUT THE RESEARCH...
A NOTE FROM CHUCK

Should people first change their thinking in order to grow as disciples, or should they first change their behavior in order to grow as disciples? The answer is not either/or, but both. In the field of neuroscience, mental processes have been found to be both a cause and effect of behavioral change. The human brain's capacity to change—called neuroplasticity—is amazing. We now know that learning new tasks can cause changes in brain activity, as well as changes in brain activity that lead to learning new tasks.[4]

By implication, learning new behaviors, such as those associated with becoming and making disciples, can lead to changes in the way we think about discipleship. But continuing in old habits can actually interfere with the thinking necessary for growth as a disciple. Perhaps this research pinpoints why discipleship has been hindered.

Behaving our way into thinking can be just as important as thinking our way into behaving. The apostle Paul is an example of someone who experienced this dual formation process— immediately changing his behavior as he grew in his understanding of discipleship and immediately changing his thinking as he perfected his behavior as a disciple.

When we strip away our cultural assumptions about what it means to be a disciple and what it means to make disciples— and *then* return to look only at the Scripture—a very different picture often emerges. We have so many misconceptions about discipleship that it's hard to know where to begin. In this chapter, we'll walk through some big paradigm shifts.

Shift #1: Jesus started making disciples in the harvest, not in the temple. Consider where Jesus found his disciples. He didn't go to the temple and wait for believers to come to him. He looked for his disciples in the harvest: in the markets, at the seashore, behind the tax-collection booths. Jesus' future disciples weren't especially religious at the time he found them; they were just regular people going about their day-to-day lives—fishing, trading, and making a living.

Jesus went to the harvest, not the temple, when looking for people to disciple. We should follow suit. We should look to disciple people at shopping malls, little league soccer games, beauty salons and barber shops, fitness clubs, coffee shops, and PTA meetings—any place where we naturally encounter people. Instead, we often do the opposite: We look almost exclusively inside the church for people who are already religious. We are looking in the wrong place for people to disciple.

Remember the man who wanted to justify himself, and so asked Jesus, "And who is my neighbor?"(Luke 10:29)? How did Jesus respond? He told him the story of the Good Samaritan—a man whom the religious people of his day would have passed by, if not consciously despised. Our neighbors are not just those who share our religion already. We are to love and serve across religious lines.

Today, this means reaching out beyond those who are like us, beyond the walls of the church, into the harvest—to serve and love our neighbor. Jesus demonstrated that approach. We should follow suit.

Shift #2: The discipleship journey starts before conversion, not after conversion. Not only did Jesus go to the people in the harvest, he also invited them to begin following him—*literally following him*—*before* they believed. That invitation was part of their journey of discipleship: Taste and see.

This observation leads us to the second misconception: Discipleship starts after people come to faith. In fact, the full journey of following Jesus starts much earlier than conversion. When we think about our own stories, we see that God uses the experiences of our lives pre-conversion as part of how he reaches us. He has been planting seeds all along the way, and that's part of our personal story.

**IF YOU CARE ABOUT THE RESEARCH...
A NOTE FROM CHUCK**

It's possible to look at how people come to faith in terms of a "bounded set" versus a "centered set."[5] A bounded set means that either you're in or you're out. There's a boundary. Looking at the process of how people come to faith, many have viewed it as a bounded set: You're in, or you're out. That certainly reflects the reality of some conversion experiences, such as the apostle Paul's. The focus of attention, then, is on getting people to receive Jesus as their savior, to confess with their mouth that Jesus Christ is Lord, and to commit to him at a fixed point in time that transfers them from outside the bounded set to inside the bounded set. The person then is no longer hell-bound, but heaven-bound.

The downside of this way of thinking is that it doesn't focus on the rest of the life of following Jesus and what that looks like. Following Jesus is a goal that you accomplish. Once you're in, you're done.

The other way to look at how people come to faith is a centered-set approach. In this case, there's more of a continuum, more of a process. The question is not whether you're in or you're out. It's: Where are you in relationship to Jesus? Are you far away or close? And which direction are you moving—away from him or toward him? In this case, our role is to encourage people along their journey, to help them move closer and closer to Jesus. Now, at some point along that journey, of course, they pass from darkness to light. They become a part of the family of God. But we (and they) don't always know exactly when that happens. We cannot necessarily identify a fixed point in time.

Just as Jesus called people to take the next step closer to him, we can also encourage people to move closer to him—even people who don't yet fully understand Jesus or aren't yet sure if they believe in him. We don't have to focus only on the finish line, but recognize all movement toward Jesus as the positive engagement that it is.

The idea that discipleship starts before conversion flies in the face of our cultural understandings. We tend to compartmentalize the journey—first evangelism, then conversion, then discipleship. That may be true in some ways, but in our day-to-day reality they often blur together more than that. Our working definition of discipleship begins with our very first encounter with Jesus. Even though we may not technically be disciples at that point, it's still an important part of our journey of discipleship.

> *Our working definition of discipleship begins with our very first encounter with Jesus. Even though we may not technically be disciples at that point, it's still an important part of our journey of discipleship.*

Consider the following examples from Scripture:
One of the criminals who hung there hurled insults at him: "Aren't you the Messiah? Save yourself and us!" But

the other criminal rebuked him. "Don't you fear God," he said, "since you are under the same sentence? We are punished justly, for we are getting what our deeds deserve. But this man has done nothing wrong." Then he said, "Jesus, remember me when you come into your kingdom." Jesus answered him, "Truly I tell you, today you will be with me in paradise" (Luke 23:39-43).

When Jesus had entered Capernaum, a centurion came to him, asking for help. "Lord," he said, "my servant lies at home paralyzed, suffering terribly." Jesus said to him, "Shall I come and heal him?" The centurion replied, "Lord, I do not deserve to have you come under my roof. But just say the word, and my servant will be healed. For I myself am a man under authority, with soldiers under me. I tell this one, 'Go,' and he goes; and that one, 'Come,' and he comes. I say to my servant, 'Do this,' and he does it." When Jesus heard this, he was amazed and said to those following him, "Truly I tell you, I have not found anyone in Israel with such great faith . . . " Then Jesus said to the centurion, "Go! Let it be done just as you believed it would." And his servant was healed at that moment (Matthew 8:5-10, 13).

As he walked along, he saw Levi son of Alphaeus sitting at the tax collector's booth. "Follow me," Jesus told him, and Levi got up and followed him. While Jesus was having dinner at Levi's house, many tax collectors and sinners were eating with him and his disciples, for there were many who followed him. When the teachers of the law who were Pharisees saw him eating with the sinners and tax collectors, they asked his disciples: "Why does he eat with tax collectors and sinners?" (Mark 2:14-16).

Sometimes the faith precedes the knowledge. When we come to Jesus, we bring with us what we have done, who we have been, and the people we have relationships with. All of this is part of our story that God can redeem and use as part of our journey of discipleship.

Sometimes the faith precedes the knowledge.

Did the criminal's history of wrongdoing, as he too died on the cross, play a part in his casting himself fully on the grace of Jesus? Yes. Did the centurion's experience of a position of power play a part in his understanding of the authority of Jesus? Yes. Were Levi's friendships with tax collectors and sinners part of his experience of coming to Jesus? Yes.

Let's look at the apostle Paul before, during, and after conversion:

Before:
At this they covered their ears and, yelling at the top of their voices, they all rushed at him, dragged him out of the city and began to stone him. Meanwhile, the witnesses laid their coats at the feet of a young man named Saul (Acts 7:57–58).

During:
Meanwhile, Saul was still breathing out murderous threats against the Lord's disciples. He went to the high priest and asked him for letters to the synagogues in Damascus, so that if he found any there who belonged to the Way, whether men or women, he might take them as prisoners to Jerusalem. As he neared Damascus on his journey, suddenly a light from heaven flashed around him. He fell to the ground and heard a voice say to him, "Saul, Saul, why do you persecute me?" (Acts 9:1–4).

After:
If someone else thinks they have reasons to put confidence in the flesh, I have more: circumcised on the eighth day, of the people of Israel, of the tribe of Benjamin,

a Hebrew of Hebrews; in regard to the law, a Pharisee; as for zeal, persecuting the church; as for righteousness based on the law, faultless. But whatever were gains to me I now consider loss for the sake of Christ. What is more, I consider everything a loss because of the surpassing worth of knowing Christ Jesus my Lord, for whose sake I have lost all things (Philippians 3:4-8).

What impact did Paul's personal history—lineage, education, pharisaism, persecution of believers, etc.—have on his later perspectives and ministry? A very great impact indeed. All of us have personal stories. God uses our stories to form us into disciples, and those stories do not begin at conversion.

> *God uses our stories to form us into disciples, and those stories do not begin at conversion.*

Therefore, we are to interact with people pre-conversion and begin discipling behaviors with them where they are. All that's needed on their end is openness—some type of response. Ask people questions, and let them ask you questions. Let them get to know you, and explain what Jesus means to you. After all, formation and mission are inextricably linked. *Keep* them integrated, from the very beginning.

As people process the message of Jesus, don't pressure them; let them take their time. God is at work, and it's him who makes the seed grow, not us (1 Corinthians 3:6-9).

IF YOU CARE ABOUT THE RESEARCH...
A NOTE FROM CHUCK

Christian psychologists Warren Brown and Brad Strawn describe the nature of the discipleship journey for most people:

"Although most Christian conversions are not as dramatic as Paul's experience on the Damascus road, nevertheless there are stories in most Christian communities of dramatic and relatively sudden conversions, after which the person is notably different in many ways. In some way, God revealed, the gospel was comprehended, and the person was changed. However, most adult formation and change is more progressive and more difficult to discern on a day-to-day basis. Significant change takes months, years, or even decades. Even relatively sudden conversions are not totally out of the blue, but are the culmination of a period of more subtle, subliminal change and formation in the individual. What is more, a critical single conversion event must be followed by months and years of progressive incorporation of the implication of the conversion into the personhood of the convert. Such was certainly the case with Paul."[6]

Shift #3: We don't need to become mature ourselves before we can start discipling others. One of the biggest misconceptions about discipleship today is that we need to be fully mature before we can start discipling others. We should wait and get our personal spiritual growth together first. After all, we can't guide where we haven't been, right?

That's probably true, but only in a very limited sense. If there are one hundred steps on the path of faith and we are only on step three, we can still lead those on steps one and two. To illustrate, let's look at a very simple, yet very important, passage:

Andrew, Simon Peter's brother, was one of the two who heard what John had said and who had followed Jesus. The first thing Andrew did was to find his brother Simon and tell him, "We have found the Messiah" (that is, the Christ). And he brought him to Jesus (John 1:40–42).

Andrew had just heard about Jesus. He was not a committed, mature follower. He certainly didn't have all of his theology straight. On paper, Andrew had zero qualifications for leading someone else along the path of faith. Yet *the first thing Andrew did* was to find his brother, tell him about Jesus, and bring him along to follow Jesus, too.

There is also the reality that every person's journey of faith is a little bit different. For instance, some of us will deal with cancer at some point, while others of us won't. Does that mean that the person who has not dealt with cancer can have nothing to say to the one who has? Of course not.

God often uses us to speak into the lives of others on issues we haven't personally lived through. We make ourselves available to others so that God can use us in whatever ways he chooses—whether we have it all together or not.

If we want to wait until we are fully mature in Christ to start making disciples, we're going to be waiting a mighty long time. And think of all the opportunities we're missing in the meantime! Rather, we are all to make disciples all the time, as we are able. Even brand-new believers can start making disciples as they're growing as disciples themselves. Discipleship is for everyone; there's no waiting period.

> *Even brand-new believers can start making disciples as they're growing as disciples themselves.*

Shift #4: We cannot separate evangelism and discipleship.
The flipside of not waiting for maturity until we make disciples is that making disciples actually helps us grow toward maturity. Consider: What will our growth look like while we are *not* making disciples? If we aren't living in obedience to what Jesus already told us to do—to make disciples—that is hardly an indication that we are on a productive path to maturity.

Personal spiritual growth and disciplemaking are simultaneous, fueling each other as we engage in both. As we continue to grow in the knowledge and grace of God, learning more about him and living and loving like Jesus did, we will be engaging in making disciples—all at the same time.

Furthermore, we cannot separate evangelism and discipleship. We need to engage in evangelism to grow in our discipleship. And we need to keep growing in our discipleship to effectively reach out to others. Both are the responsibility of all believers: to be disciples, and to make disciples.

Too many people just try to get people saved as opposed to following Jesus for their whole lives. But Jesus is calling us into a relationship with himself that lasts throughout life. We do people a major disservice when we artificially separate salvation from a lifelong relationship with God. Rather than only pressing for conversion decisions, we should connect authentically with people and share the good news of the gospel of grace.

Even though we may not be especially gifted in sharing our faith, we can spend time in the harvest and encounter people in our natural networks. Opportunities are plentiful for investing in the lives of nonbelievers, becoming a part of their spiritual journeys, and helping them transition into Christ-followers. All believers have the responsibility to make disciples, and we don't fully grow in our own discipleship unless we're engaging authentically with those who don't yet know Jesus.

IF YOU CARE ABOUT THE RESEARCH...
A NOTE FROM CHUCK

The assumed separation of evangelism and discipleship is based on the semantic principle known as *bivalence*.[7] Here a proposition has one truth value: Either the proposition is true, or it is false. Based on this line of reasoning, Christians often imply the following proposition: Evangelism and discipleship are separate activities. Therefore, evangelism is not discipleship, and discipleship is not evangelism.

However, the problem lies in the ambiguity and vagueness of common usages of the words *evangelism* and *discipleship*. A word is ambiguous when it can be assigned multiple meanings, and a word is vague when it is inexplicit and imprecise. Essentially, there can be overlap, or one could be a subset of another. In ordinary discourse, we tend to overlook the process of transformation that is common ground to both evangelism and discipleship, making our typical definitions of these terms conceptually flawed. Therefore, only the most arbitrary judgments are made about where evangelism ends and discipleship begins.

Based on a critical examination of scripture, Roy Moran challenges the contemporary view that implies the separation of evangelism from discipleship.

No Exceptions for Pastors

It shouldn't have to be said, but it does: There is no exception clause for pastors. It's not as if pastors are only to galvanize others to reach out into the harvest to make disciples. We are to do it ourselves as well. As in all other things, we lead by example.

Whatever people see the pastor doing is what they will do. While traveling in Honduras, Bob noticed that pastors are very involved in reaching new people who are not already followers of Jesus. The situation reminded Bob of the old lay preachers, always pressing on to the next place to preach the gospel and see new churches raised up. Having the pastors involved in that activity was just a cultural given in Honduras. Consequently, the people are involved as well.

As pastors, our actions speak louder than our words. If our people see us doing something, they think it must be important. Conversely, if we are not doing something, they decide that it must be optional or unimportant. There is no substitute for personal engagement in the harvest if you're a pastor.

What Do We *Really* Believe?

These paradigm shifts are challenging for most of us. They fly in the face of what we have been taught about evangelism and discipleship. Yet when we look at Scripture, they line up. Reflect on the following points that have been made in this chapter and consider to what degree you really believe them or not:

- All believers are called to make disciples of others.
- The work of discipleship starts in the harvest, not at conversion.
- Our own story of discipleship started before we came to faith.
- Even new Christians can reach out and begin discipling others—there is no waiting period.
- As we walk alongside people who are not yet Christians, we can engage in pre-discipleship as they move toward Jesus.
- We don't need to wait to become mature ourselves before we can start discipling others.
- We cannot separate making disciples and living as disciples—they are simultaneous and they fuel each other.
- We cannot become mature ourselves until we start making disciples.

"That was some assignment, Jim. This has been a week of rethinking some long-standing paradigms I've had—everything from what it means to be a pastor to the very nature of discipleship! Not to mention some serious soul-searching. You know what I realized?"

"What?"

"That I'm expecting the people in my congregation to do things I'm not doing myself. I've been expecting them to reach out to their friends and neighbors with the gospel, while exempting myself from that same standard. Because I'm a pastor, I've been expecting people to come to me to become disciples instead of me going to them and meeting them where they are—outside the church. It's been an eye-opening week."

"What are you going to do about it?" asked Jim.

Rob smiled. "I'm going to take up snowshoeing again."

"Come again?" Jim looked puzzled.

"It's funny really," explained Rob. "I've been putting off exercising since I've been so busy with work at the church. And I used to love snowshoeing. So I'm going to start back up again with a few guys from around town who are into it—especially now that we're looking at getting a lot of snow over the next few months. I don't know them very well yet—seems like I haven't found the time to develop as many relationships outside of the church—but they're guys I would like to spend more time with. Oh, and I'm also going to start volunteering at my kids' school—something else I thought I didn't have time for because I was too busy with ministry." Rob smiled. "Ironic, isn't it?"

CHAPTER 4

DISCERNING WHAT'S NEXT IN YOUR DISCIPLESHIP JOURNEY

"The usual?" asked the barista, as Rob stepped into the coffee shop, snowflakes in his hair and on his coat. The employees and regulars at the coffee shop knew them by now, and it was nice to be welcomed with a smile and a nod of recognition.

Rob found he was feeling better as he waited for Jim to arrive—less stressed-out and more connected to the community around him. He greeted the barista by name and asked how his girlfriend was. It was nice to feel like there was less of a wall between the people from church and the people in the surrounding neighborhood.

Rob was sure the exercise was helping with his attitude, but there was something else too. Rob found he was feeling less pressure to make something happen, and more of a sense that God would bring about what he wanted to bring about. He had always associated that attitude with laziness and a do-nothing approach, but that wasn't it at all. He was actually now more active in following God's commands, not less. But rather than feeling responsible for the results, he was able to leave them more in God's hands. It was refreshing.

Jim walked in the door, shivering a bit. "I'm not used to these northern winters."

Rob laughed. "This is not bad as winters here go, actually. I think what you're used to is living near the equator!"

"You know what occurred to me after our last meeting, Rob? You needed a map."

"I'm pretty sure I know how far north of the equator we are now."

"No, I meant for your own personal discipleship," explained Jim. "On your diagram, you had the categories all there—where you wanted to go. But until you knew your own personal starting point—what you needed to work on—you weren't able to figure out how to get there."

"Well, I still haven't exactly gotten there," admitted Rob. "I mean, I've gotten to know the people who work here at this coffee shop. But in my engagement with people who don't know Jesus, what I'm mostly learning so far is that I have a long way to go."

"That's okay. As long as you don't give up. From what I've seen, pastors often have a lot of work to do in this area. Both pastors and church attenders need to have natural relationships with people outside the church. And if it starts with you, it's more likely to be passed along to those you're leading. My point here is that you needed to know that—you needed to know your starting point."

Jim looked out the window at the bare branches of the trees shaking in the wind, and continued. "It reminds me of when I was lost driving around in the middle-of-nowhere Texas. I had a map in my truck, but a fat lot of good it did me when I'd come to these rural intersections with no road signs posted. You have to first figure out where you are on the map before you can figure out what direction you need to go."

"Who uses maps anymore?" laughed Rob. "I have a GPS on my phone. There's a little blue dot on my phone that tells me where I am, and a little red dot that tells me where I'm going. I can even get a little blue line showing me the whole way there. It's not possible to get lost."

"Sure it is. What happens when you lose cell reception? That little blue dot disappears." Jim raised his eyebrows, "I may be seventy-four, but I'm familiar with the technology." He smiled. "I know you can still see the map on your phone—at least where it froze when you went out of range—but you don't know where you are on it anymore."

"A fair point. That's happened when I've driven into the mountains. What does this have to do with discipleship again?"

"A map isn't enough. People have to know where they are on it. You needed to know you weren't strong in the area of reaching out before you decided to do something about it. Other people need the same thing. Before they can come up with a good discipleship strategy, they also need to assess where they already are in relation to it. Where are their strengths? Where are their weaknesses? What areas have they not given much consideration to thus far? What are

they sensing from God? Then they can get direction for their own discipleship."

Rob frowned as he considered the issue. "Hmmm. I think you're right. And I think maybe it's time to go back to the little test-group at my church that helped me come up with the tree in the first place. Maybe together we can do a bit of assessment to figure out where we are in our discipleship journey so far."

Let's begin this chapter by debunking an influential and pervasive myth—that our discipleship growth is "just me and God." Especially in the western church, we have incorporated a spirit of individualism into our walk of faith that simply isn't there in the scriptures. This seems to reflect the values of our individualistic culture—pulling ourselves up by our own boot-straps—which has subtly seeped into the church.

When we look at the Scriptures, we see Nathan providing a sharp challenge to King David (2 Samuel 12). We see Mordecai pushing Esther to do the right thing (Esther 4). We see Paul publicly correcting Peter in an error (Galatians 2). In short, we see not only general encouragement, but people speaking directly into one another's lives.

We cannot afford to ignore the significant others around us who can speak into our lives in meaningful ways. They have a perspective that we don't—a perspective that we need.

We cannot afford to ignore the significant others around us who can speak into our lives in meaningful ways.

On the other hand, in some cultures around the world, people will not provide unsolicited feedback. This especially seems to reflect the values of collectivistic cultures, in which people in authority are assumed to go unquestioned. That means we will need to ask for feedback. There are many ways we can do that, both formally and informally, but one helpful method is a discipleship assessment. A good assessment can line up each of the qualities of a holistic disciple, and then guide us and those who know us well to reflect on how we currently measure up to these qualities.

Most of us are feeling more than a little uncomfortable right now. What if we don't measure up very well? Let's remove the element of surprise right now: We won't. None of us will. The point of a discipleship assessment is to pinpoint areas for growth. Scripture requires honesty of us:

> Do not think of yourself more highly than you ought, but rather think of yourself with sober judgment, in accordance with the faith God has distributed to each of you (Romans 12:3).

We are not to think of ourselves more highly—or more lowly—than we ought, but with accurate and sober judgment. We all need some times when we take a good look in the mirror, evaluate ourselves with sober judgment, and measure ourselves against the life of discipleship that God has laid out for us in the Scriptures. A refusal to look honestly at our own lives is tantamount to choosing blindness, and leads to a posture of judgmentalism toward others:

> Why do you look at the speck of sawdust in your brother's eye and pay no attention to the plank in your own eye? How can you say to your brother, "Let me take the speck out of your eye," when all the time there is a plank in your own eye? (Matthew 7:3-4).

Let us not be the kind of people who glance in the mirror and then immediately forget what we look like (James 1:24). Instead, let us be the kind of people who are unafraid to look honestly at ourselves and the way we live our lives as disciples of Jesus. It takes courage, but it is the more honest way to live, and it gives us sure footing on the path of discipleship.

A sober assessment can be an effective tool for gauging and monitoring the process of disciplemaking. It can help us see where we are, where we want to go, and how we might create a plan to get there. But that starts with looking in the mirror and taking stock of where we currently are on our journey of discipleship.

THE CHARACTERISTICS OF A SOBER ASSESSMENT

Many of us do not know what a sober assessment entails, even if we recognize its importance. How can we go about getting an assessment of where we are in our discipleship journey that is complete, impartial, and accurate? What qualities make an assessment effective? It should be:

Reliable: Measuring with the right yardstick or scale to ensure that our measurement is accurate and consistent
Valid: Knowing what we want to measure and measuring the right things
Fair: Assessing in a way that allows various groups to be evaluated on equal footing
Practical: Presenting the information yielded by the assessment in a way that it is useful, makes sense, and doesn't bog people down in difficult-to-interpret language
Formative: As opposed to coming to a conclusion, the results of an assessment point toward a process of change and ongoing growth.

**IF YOU CARE ABOUT THE RESEARCH...
A NOTE FROM CHUCK**

The overall soundness of assessments is covered in the field known as psychometric theory (the study of tests and measurements). While all five of the characteristics discussed in this chapter are essential to high-quality assessment, reliability and validity are considered the two most basic components.[8]

Reliable

An assessment being reliable means that we are measuring with an instrument that ensures our results are accurate and consistent. Imagine a person's actual weight is 160 pounds. One day he steps on the scale and it reads 162. The next day it reads 159, even though his actual weight has not changed since the day before. That scale is unreliable.

Conversely, let's say that same person gains three pounds over a two-week period, but the scale still says 160. Again, the assessment instrument—in this case, the scale—is unreliable. A reliable assessment is one that yields accurate, consistent results.

When it comes to the area of measuring our discipleship, we should probably begin by admitting that we are not always the most accurate judges of ourselves. Anyone who is married knows this. Our spouse sees things about us that we have never noticed—and points them out. Our usual response is, "What's wrong with that? Everyone does that. It's no big deal." Or even, "I did not recognize that about myself." The problem is that all of us are using ourselves as a benchmark for what's normal. In reality, each one of us is different, and all of us have blind spots.

Even when we're trying our best to be honest, we have a limited perspective on what we can observe. In studies of events such as car accidents, interviewers ask witnesses what they saw. They might ask fifteen people, and all fifteen will report a slightly different version of events. That's not necessarily because any of the witnesses are intentionally lying; they just all saw the accident from a different perspective. They were each paying attention to certain details and missed others. Their pre-accident mental state also may have influenced their perceptions. Yet the accident only happened one way. Therefore, a composite of their perspectives usually gives us the clearest picture.

This dynamic is similar to the way the four gospels were written. Some are more detailed, some more poetic, some faster-paced, some geared toward different audiences. Yet the life of Jesus only happened one way. Does that mean that only one of the gospels is accurate? Not at all. They all represent different perspectives, and taken together give us the most accurate representation—a composite.

It's more reliable, and more biblical, to get multiple perspectives. If we self-evaluate, that's just one perspective and therefore more likely to be inaccurate. Hearing from more people who know us well gives us a clearer picture of where we're at. We all have our unique blind spots, defenses, and limitations. All human judgments are subjective at some level, but taken together they give us the most accurate composite picture. For this reason, a 360-degree assessment is much more accurate than a self-assessment.

A "360 assessment" incorporates the perspectives of other significant people in our lives— those who see us more clearly than we see ourselves. The people that God has placed around us are an invaluable resource in helping us get an accurate picture of ourselves. Therefore, a 360 assessment is conducted with a variety of people who represent our constellation of relationships: family and friends, group and team members who are peers, our spiritual leaders, people we are leading or discipling, and of course, ourselves.

**IF YOU CARE ABOUT THE RESEARCH...
A NOTE FROM CHUCK**

What is a 360-degree assessment? A "360 assessment" includes the perspectives of peers, supervisors, and subordinates as well as ourselves. The most important benefit of a 360-degree assessment is its potential for reliability. The collective perspectives of many people tend to converge on the most accurate portrayals of a person, while simultaneously canceling out the inaccurate portrayals.[9]

Valid

In addition to using a reliable assessment instrument, we also need to be sure we are using a valid one. Being valid means that the instrument is measuring the attribute it's supposed to measure. If you step on the scale, and it's supposed to measure weight but gives you height, that's not a valid scale. It may be reliable, in the sense that it's giving you an accurate height, but it's not valid because height wasn't what you were trying to measure.

Many of the ways we try to assess our discipleship are invalid because we aren't clear on what we are aiming for. What *is* a disciple? This is the question we addressed in Chapter 2.

With any type of assessment, it's important to make sure we are measuring the right things. People's perspectives need to be grounded in something precise and observable. For this reason, it's best to measure specific behaviors rather than vague qualities that are open to greater misinterpretation. The real test of discipleship is the degree to which we live out what we do know to be true.

For God, who said, "Let light shine out of darkness," made his light shine in our hearts to give us the light of the knowledge of God's glory displayed in the face of Christ (2 Corinthians 4:6).

That's transformation: the display of Jesus to those around us in a way that they can see it. Inner qualities can only be seen through behaviors. Behaviors can be measured through words and deeds. Discipleship is not simply about what we believe, but about how we live. How we live reflects what we truly believe. For this reason, a good assessment doesn't measure how important a person thinks reaching out to others is, but to what degree she engages in it.

> *Discipleship is not simply about what we believe, but about how we live.*

We also need to be sure to measure the right actions—actions that are indicative of character. Let's be clear: Measuring the wrong actions makes an assessment invalid.

One question might read, "To what degree do you see [name of disciple] forgiving others and asking for forgiveness?" A scale of 1–5 is given. Others can then give you feedback on what they see you doing—or on what they don't see. In this way we honor the subjectivity of various perspectives, but at the same time ground it in behavioral observations.

How can we establish validity when it comes to discipleship? We can do it by culling our profile of a disciple from Scripture, getting help and input from subject-matter experts in those areas, and by grounding our observations in measurable behaviors. Taking steps like these will help us ensure that we are measuring the right things.

Fair

Besides ensuring that our assessment is reliable and valid, we must make every effort to ensure that our assessment is fair. Fairness means that our instruments and procedures for gathering and interpreting information are valid for the various groups being assessed.

**IF YOU CARE ABOUT THE RESEARCH...
A NOTE FROM CHUCK**

Imagine an assessment that tends to yield one pattern of information for African Americans and another for Caucasians. Robert Williams designed just such an assessment.[10] His purpose in designing the test was to call attention to the racial bias in standard intelligence tests—one that favors white middle-class values. The language used leaned heavily on black cultural linguis-

---

tic references—vocabulary and phrases unfamiliar to most whites. Not surprisingly, African Americans scored much higher on this particular test.

At the time, Williams wanted to make a point about language and cultural bias inherent in traditional psychological tests. In particular, he called attention to how intelligence tests favored Caucasians over African-Americans and how some social scientists used these findings as a basis for promoting theories of racial superiority and inferiority. The assessment was unfair. It made group membership—not the attributes they were attempting to measure—the basis for the results.

Any assessment that gives biased interpretations, for whatever reason, is inherently unfair. In this sense, fairness is closely aligned with validity. A sound assessment measures the target attributes accurately and consistently, and does so for individuals from different groups.

The importance of fairness is biblical. For instance, Solomon made this statement at the outset of the book of Proverbs, as he explained its purpose: "for receiving instruction on prudent behavior, doing what is right and just and fair" (Proverbs 1:3).

To be fair means to pass a right judgment on human actions, whether this means an assessment of ourselves (self-assessment) or assessment of others. No one is at an advantage or disadvantage. As Jesus said in John 7:24, "Look beneath the surface so you can judge correctly" (NLT).

Practical

In addition to being reliable, valid, and fair, a good assessment is practical. Let's say you have the most reliable and valid scale in the world. It measures weight as it's supposed to, and it measures very, very accurately. But the scale itself weighs a ton and it's so big you can't get it into the bathroom. No one can figure out how to use the complex computer interface that allows you to read the results, and when you get the results you find that you are 160.14579 pounds—most of which is not useful information. No matter how good of a scale it is, no one is going to use it. It's not practical and it's not user-friendly.

Likewise, we want an assessment instrument that doesn't require a PhD in physics to interpret the results, and we want the results to be helpful. Sometimes there's a tradeoff between reliability, validity, and practicality. Nonetheless, we want the highest reliability and validity possible, and still be given meaningful results.

The key questions for practicality are: Can we use the assessment procedure without having to climb unnecessary hurdles? Can we process the results? When we get these results, what can we do with them? If the answers are unclear, the assessment is not practical.

When we get helpful results, they lend themselves to reflection. Let's take the example of the question about forgiveness mentioned above. Five people who know you might respond that you are strong in this area—not because they made it up, but because they have observed your behavior. You then have validation about a certain aspect of your discipleship: "Yes, I am strong in this area." You suspected as much, but now you have confirmation.

In other cases, you may receive a correction that you're thinking too highly or too lowly of yourself in a specific area. Let's say an assessment asks about the degree to which you show hospitality without favoritism. You may consider yourself strong in this area, but if five other people score you low, that's feedback you need to take into consideration.

What are they seeing that you are not? Possibly there have been cases of hospitality they are not aware of. Possibly you are thinking too highly of yourself in this area. The reverse may be true as well. You may score yourself low in hospitality, while several others all score you high. A similar question needs to be asked: What are they seeing that you are not?

Honesty is paramount as you consider feedback gathered from an assessment. You must allow enough flexibility for the Holy Spirit to lead; and to do that, you must remain open to seeing yourself through different eyes. Pray for openness in your spirit and look for patterns in the feedback you are receiving.

One interesting pattern that sometimes occurs is the mixed response. Let's say the assessment asked about your level of relational transparency as you walk alongside others through life challenges. Your peers and spiritual leaders may rate you high in this area, while those you lead or are discipling may rate you low. Is there something that leads you to share your weaknesses with one group, but not with the other?

Now that you have the hard data, you can get feedback from individuals in the various groups. Ask them for specific observations of your behavior that led them to rate you as they did. Perhaps you might find that you behave differently depending on the group. And what might this say about your character as a disciple?

By considering the feedback you receive from various groups of people, you can gain a clearer picture of your own walk of discipleship. Results from a practical assessment give you the information you need to help you grow and move forward—which brings us to the fourth characteristic of a good assessment: being formative.

Formative

A formative assessment is one that you continue to use to make progress over time. (Its opposite is a summative assessment: one that gives an unchanging and unchangeable conclusion.) You might think of it as the difference between getting a degree and being a lifelong learner.

Something that is formative isn't all-or-nothing. It's not either being exactly where you want to be or nowhere at all. People can be hard on themselves, so we need to affirm both the progress made and the effort that needs to go into that progress. The question isn't whether we've made it there or not, but what small steps we can take to get more traction in that direction. Note that this perspective applies to both the discipler and the "disciplee."

Ideally, then, a formative assessment is taken regularly like an annual physical. You go in to the doctor, identify your strong points, and learn ways you can improve your health and your quality of life. A discipleship assessment is a similar way of growing in the spiritual realm.

In an "annual spiritual" (like an annual physical), it's important to start by affirming strengths. None of us are motivated by seeing that we have a huge amount of work to do and have made no progress so far. The truth is, we likely *have* made progress. Our strengths also indicate that we have something to give, something to contribute that the world needs.

Then, after identifying strengths, we can pinpoint growth areas. How can we continue to become more like Jesus over time? We are never finished, always growing.

Like a series of snapshots, we can chart our growth over a period of time. Some parents have a tradition of taking a photo of their child on the first day of school every year. Each of those snapshots shows just one particular point in time. But the resulting record of all of them shows incremental growth and change over the course of the years. A formative assessment is not just about product but about process. It is the evolving picture of us over time.

A formative assessment is not just about product but about process. It is the evolving picture of us over time.

Of course, assessment scores aren't much good if we don't do anything with them. Short of direct, blinded-by-the-light supernatural intervention, growth doesn't generally just happen without some intentionality. We do our part, and God does his.

The more deliberate and intentional we can be about our own journey of discipleship, the more likely we are to grow in it. In most cases, we don't grow due to lack of intentionality. We are not doing our part, but waiting for God to do all of it. A tended field produces more fruit than an untended one.

A good assessment gives us the right starting point. But knowing where we are is only useful if we're planning to go somewhere. We need to do something with the results, and a good assessment will provide us with possible directions for future growth.

Knowing where we are is only useful if we're planning to go somewhere.

We need guidance from the Holy Spirit as we look at our assessment results. What are others saying about us? What resonates? What are we hearing from God? It's a humbling process to have to rely on God and others, but it's one we need to engage in if we are to move forward in our growth.

Honest and prayerful reflection precedes action planning. Only after we have spent time listening to God and others and reflecting on what we are hearing should we move forward with a course of action. Then we can identify our starting point and create a plan for moving forward.

So Why Don't We Do It?

That's the question, isn't it? It's one thing to know what makes for an effective assessment; it's another thing entirely to take it. Like going to the doctor for our annual physical, it's something we often put off doing. Why?

Here are some common blockages to taking a sober assessment of our discipleship, followed by an opportunity to do some self-assessment about those blockages:

Not wanting to know. This blockage is similar to not wanting to get on the scale. It's a fear of getting feedback. What if someone shares something negative? Simply put, we don't want to feel bad.

Not a priority. Taking a sober assessment of our discipleship requires some time and commitment. It requires an investment of some kind on our part. Since we have limited time, energy, and money, we choose to invest it in areas we consider more important.

Not necessary. Many times people work under the assumption that a formal assessment isn't necessary. If we go to church, or have a quiet time, or are involved in a small group, then we must be growing. There's no need to look more carefully.

Not recognizing the need. While some people do not think a formal assessment is necessary, others do not even consider its need. As they scurry on with the business of ministry, blind to who they really are, they do not stop and ask themselves an important question: "How would a clear and sober picture of myself help in my development as a disciple?"

Not helpful. Sometimes people simply don't think an assessment will be helpful. What would it accomplish? This blockage is similar to a husband or wife saying, "Therapy won't help my marriage," and often comes from people who have tried something in the past that hasn't been effective.

Not having a good instrument. Unfortunately, some of the assessment tools used in ministry do not hold to the standards of reliability, validity, and practicality. Even with our good intentions in using them, they may not yield the type of data that enables us to grow and develop. (Note: We have developed an assessment called the Dimensions of Discipleship, based on the tree diagram in the preceding chapter, which can be found at discipleshipdifference.com.)

No clear goal. When there is no clear picture of what the outcome is supposed to look like—no standard to measure oneself against—people are unlikely to engage in an assessment. If our picture of a disciple is vague, what is there to assess?

Desire to avoid accountability. If people get results from an assessment, they are accountable to do something with those results. One way to avoid accountability is to not take the assessment in the first place.

Which of these blockages do you see in your context?

_____

_____

_____

_____

How might you best address them?

_____

_____

_____

_____

GETTING THE BIGGER PICTURE

We've seen in this chapter how assessment is integral to growing disciples. Individuals can get an accurate snapshot of where they are at one point in time, and get data on how they can continue to grow in their discipleship journey.

Yet discipleship assessments have value not just for individuals, but for whole communities as well. Say your whole congregation took assessments. What data might that yield? You would receive individual scores for each person, but you may also be able to see composite results. Using the data in this manner could give you a discipleship profile of your church, as well as of profiles of individuals within the church. You may notice that a particular area is low, say, generous living or authentic relationships. That kind of information can help you know how to move your church forward in such a way that will help people grow.

On the other hand, you may notice an area of relative strength, such as sacrificial service and community transformation. That kind of information can be used as affirmation and encouragement to the people in your church. It also adds balance to the bigger picture of how your church is doing overall in its discipleship.

Imagine how such feedback could help you strengthen whole churches and ministries by focusing energy on the areas where the Spirit is leading you toward growth. By looking at composite results, you can measure overall trends in discipleship across ministries, across congregations, across denominations, and throughout the church worldwide. The potential impact of sober assessments is significant.

> *By looking at composite results, you can measure overall trends in discipleship across ministries, across congregations, across denominations, and throughout the church worldwide.*

The group of key leaders gathered in the church classroom where the discipleship class had been held. The old radiators clicked and sputtered as people wandered in: Jack and Elsa, who had been running the kids' Sunday school program as long as anyone could remember. Laurel, the veterinary technician, who put together social events for the teens and talked with them about God along the way. Stan, who led one of the stronger small groups. Caroline, the part-time worship director, and full-time music teacher at a nearby college. Burt and Gracie, who were simply always around, and therefore indispensable to the life of First Community Church.

These were Rob's key leaders. Eight people, including himself. They spent the day reflecting on their discipleship journeys, both together and individually. They prayed and asked questions of one another. They gave each other honest feedback. They engaged in self-reflection, open to the possibility of what God might want to do among them.

CHAPTER 5

THE MOSAIC PROCESS OF DISCIPLESHIP

"Nice advice, Jim. That didn't work at all," said Rob, exasperated. Jim just warmed his hands on his steaming cup of coffee and waited for him to continue.

"We were supposed to find out where we need to focus our discipleship efforts as a church. I was hoping it would become clear what branch of the tree to zero in on. But no. The takeaways were completely scattered. Burt senses God's leading in the area of generous living. Caroline wants to focus on community transformation. Laurel didn't pick a branch at all, but feels what's important is the trunk of the tree—how we respond to what we're hearing from God. Jack senses a need for more evangelism and has proposed a new Vacation Bible School program. Stan thinks I should be telling them what to focus on since I'm the pastor." Rob put his head down and ran his fingers through his hair. "That group of people couldn't agree on the color of the sanctuary carpet."

"This is getting really messy," he continued, looking up. "I was hoping this time of discernment would give me direction—a sermon series on, say, reading the Bible, or on relationships, or on outreach, or on generosity. But these people are scattered all over the place. So where does that leave us? I honestly don't see how any kind of curriculum could cover it all in a coherent way."

"True," agreed Jim. "Discipleship is messy. And people never seem to want to address things in the nice linear fashion you've laid out for them. May as well work with the messiness, I'm thinking." Rob waited for him to clarify, but instead, Jim started to tell a story from his time on the mission field.

"When I was serving in Honduras, travel was difficult and technology was almost non-existent. Many of the methods we use here to organize and oversee discipleship simply didn't exist there: no email, few telephones, no large worship services, no advertising. Most of the pastors were also farmers on the side, and had second or third-grade formal educations at best.

"Yet people were telling each other about Jesus. Then those people were telling others about their newfound faith. Believers were multiplying and small church gatherings were multiplying throughout these small jungle villages. The Spirit was at work and the people were cooperating.

"You know what kind of discipleship curriculum we used? You'll be amazed at its flexibility and elasticity. When a new believer began to follow Christ, the church would baptize that person immediately. The church followed the approach described in Acts: They believed, were baptized, and were added to the church. This practice was different than in most Latin American countries where lengthy catechism or sanctification came before baptism. After the new converts' baptisms, while they were still dripping wet—this was a Baptist group I was with, after all!—the follow-up began.

"First, the baptizer read from Romans 6: You died with Christ, were buried with Christ, were raised with Christ . . . The power of God that raised Jesus from the dead frees us from sin. Then the baptizer asked the first follow-up question: 'What sinful habit do you have that you need the power of the resurrected Jesus to change?' This was not a rhetorical question. An answer was expected, then and there. The new believer had already experienced the transforming power of Jesus in justification; now they needed to experience it in sanctification. And since they now had the Holy Spirit, it was assumed that they had the capacity to listen to God for themselves.

"Once an answer was given, the baptizer then asked them how the person could move forward in that area. Again, not a rhetorical question. After the person answered, they were given one passage of Scripture relevant to the stated issue. The new believer then had a plan of action on the number-one issue in their personal and character development, along with scriptural input.

"The second part of the follow-up—while still dripping wet, mind you—began with a citation from Acts 1: As you know, you are now a witness to the resurrected Christ. No training is necessary for a new believer to be a witness: It is simply a matter of testimony to what they have experienced, telling others what's happened to them. The new believer is already eminently qualified to be a witness.

"The baptizer then would ask: 'Who do you know that needs the transforming power of Jesus?' The new believer thinks of a spouse, a brother, a neighbor, etc., and is then asked what she could do to help *that person experience the transforming power of Jesus. That course of action is then linked to a passage of Scripture she can reflect on.*

"So right at the moment of coming to faith, the new follower of Christ is put on two tracks: growing personally, and serving and reaching out to others. They report back each week to the person who baptized them on what they've done and what is next. The baptizer has no other agenda or plan, but relies on the Holy Spirit to grow this new follower of Christ, trusting that he is at work in their lives.

"Out of this basic process, new believers emerge, new churches emerge, and new leaders emerge. As they tell others about their experience with Jesus and someone responds to that message, the original baptizer will ask, 'So what needs to happen next?' 'Well, I suppose they need to be baptized.' 'Yes. You know how to do that. And then what?' And the cycle continues, as they take others through the process they themselves have been through."

Rob just stared at him. "That's amazing. Let me make sure I'm understanding you right. Each person came up with their own direction for discipleship by listening to the Holy Spirit for themselves? One personal issue and one outreach issue?"

"Yes," confirmed Jim.

"Wasn't that a little early—immediately after conversion—to expect people to start reaching out and doing evangelism? I mean, shouldn't they learn some things first?" asked Rob.

"You just asked the million-dollar question. Are you sure you want me to answer it? I will need to get on my soapbox to do so."

Jim's eyes were twinkling as he said this, but Rob could tell he wasn't entirely joking.

"Permission granted to get on your soapbox."

"Your question—and the underlying assumption that we need to learn and grow first and then serve and reach out—is probably the number-one problem with the western church. The fact is, it needs to happen all at once. There needs to be a constant back-and-forth between inner growth and outward service. If we don't serve and reach out and use what we're learning, the inner growth stops.

"On the other hand," continued Jim, "when people reach out to others with the gospel message from day one, their personal growth is accelerated. I saw this over and over in Honduras. We would challenge people to immediately start loving their neighbors, not just other believers, and it was incredibly effective. People are capable of much more than we give them credit for. Outward focus from day one is crucial for development. Don't wait, or you'll never get around to it."

Rob could almost feel the pieces coming together in his mind as Jim talked. He ventured, "So for instance. . . Burt could work on generous living while reaching out to the guys in his antique car club. . . and Laurel could focus her energy on learning how to hear God's voice through Scripture while reaching out to teenagers? Everyone could be working on something completely different at the same time... and growing both inwardly and outwardly at the same time ...and that would be fine?"

"Yes. That's precisely what I mean," confirmed Jim with a nod.

Let's move more directly into how we can go about making disciples effectively. Given that God may be directing different people to work on different issues at different times, how can we move forward together, in a way that makes sense?

The first order of business is likely getting more comfortable in working with the mess. We like a one-step, two-step, three-step kind of approach—the kind you can diagram so one point flows logically to the next. However, life seldom conforms itself to such a neat pattern.

Instead, our path of faith tends to be more mosaic. Mosaic is an artistic term referring to a design made up of smaller, disparate elements that come together to form something greater than the sum of its parts. It's like a collage made up of tiny stones—each stone shaped and colored differently—but arranged together in such a way that they make a larger pattern.

Life is like that. So is discipleship. Different little pieces come into play and we often aren't really sure what they mean when we run across them. But we place one, then God places another, then we start to place new pieces based on how the earlier pieces were arranged. Eventually we see a bigger pattern taking shape.

Instead of a linear approach to discipleship, we'll explore in this chapter what a mosaic approach to discipleship can look like—something that we can arrange and rearrange as we go, taking into account our life circumstances and how God is already at work.

One important point before we dive in: Taking a mosaic approach to discipleship does *not* mean that we lose the intentionality. We are relational and flexible, taking into account what each person is hearing from God, but we continue to be relentlessly intentional about becoming the kind of disciples God wants us to be. Essentially, the goal is to individualize our approach to discipleship without losing the intentionality. We are to be flexible and intentional at the same time.

The goal is to individualize our approach to discipleship without losing the intentionality

As we disciple others, we need to keep in mind that we are not the ones in charge of the process—the Holy Spirit is. He will take things in directions we cannot imagine or plan for. Our role is to ask authentic questions and listen to his voice. From there, we follow his leading. We need to be intentional—not about following our own plan, but about listening to the leading of the Holy Spirit.

Only in the context of these intentional conversations can we discern how God is calling each one of us to grow. Through those conversations we can learn how God's agenda for me right now can be different from God's agenda for you right now—and how we can pray for and encourage one another accordingly. Consider this scenario:

> You're part of a group of believers gathering together. You're talking about what you're hearing from God. You're sensing his hand of correction in how you've not been consistent in keeping your commitments. You say, "Yes, I'll do that," and then you forget about it. You're now sensing tension around this pattern. Others speak into your life. They have seen this dynamic play out too, and they confirm that it does make for difficulties for the people around you.

> "What about your inward life?" someone asks. Lately, you have been struck lately by Jesus' heart of compassion for those around him, how he allows himself to really feel it as he sees people struggling. You would like to develop a similar heart of compassion.

> "What steps could you take in that direction?" Talking with those around you, you decide on some specific

windows of exposure to people who are hurting: spending some time in the part of town where the newly arrived refugees are trying to settle into a life that is completely different from all they have known.

"What about steps for honoring your commitments?" You have no idea, and ask for input. One comment that strikes home is that you could write down your commitments onto your calendar when you make them. That way you won't forget. That seems to be a good first step.

You receive prayer. Then you provide a listening ear and a sounding board for the others in your gathering as they process through what they are hearing from God and what next steps he might be asking them to take in their growth. You listen, provide input, and pray. You then continue to provide ongoing encouragement for one another along your very different paths of discipleship, according to what each of you are hearing from God.

This is one example of how God can be at work in a mosaic pattern. Did the other people in this group have an agenda for how you were to move forward? No. They had no idea. They simply listened, asked questions, encouraged you to follow God's leading, and prayed. This is an example of discerning and cooperating with what God is doing—and learning how to listen to the Spirit.

We all need relational support, modeling, and help—especially at the beginning of our walk of faith—but we don't need someone else controlling our process. None of us is qualified to play the role of the Holy Spirit. Rather we are to direct one another toward engaging with God for ourselves. In this way, we all increasingly take on responsibility for our own growth—while still remaining within a supportive community that encourages us along the way.

INWARD AND OUTWARD TOGETHER

You can see how the inward and the outward aspects of discipleship can be very naturally woven together in this type of discipleship. As we are growing, we are reaching out. As we are reaching out, we are growing. It comes together in a mosaic pattern when, at every step of our growth, we have both an inward focus and an outward focus, just as the new believers in the Honduras story.

It's not sequential, but simultaneous. Remember Philemon 1:6 (NIV 84): "I pray that you may be active in sharing your faith, so that you will have a full understanding of every good thing we have in Christ." We can't have a full understanding of all the good things we have in Christ unless we are active in sharing those good things.

MOVING TOWARD HOLISTIC DISCIPLESHIP

The mosaic pattern continues as we help one another move toward an integrated, holistic kind of discipleship—the kind that includes hands, head, and heart.

We all have our natural defaults, don't we? One person may emphasize the heart to the exclusion of the head and hands. Another person may be strong in head and heart, but needs to strengthen and use his or her hands to move toward maturity in the faith.

Yet all of us need all three in order to become holistic disciples of Jesus. We cannot veer to extremes, but need fullness in each of these areas. Having a supportive community around us can help us see what we cannot see on our own.

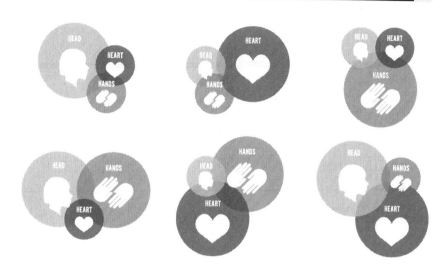

Bob shares that for years and years during his walk of discipleship, he mostly ignored the area of social justice. It just didn't fit his theological paradigm, and it didn't register that he needed to be involved personally in helping the poor. Social justice simply was not on his discipleship radar, leading to a weakness in the "hands" area.

Bob describes his process: "As I began to grow in my awareness, this became a clear growth point for me. It was transformative for me when I started to engage in this way by serving in a recovery home. I was helped as much if not more than they were helped. I began teaching an anger management class to people living at the Salvation Army, and found that I learned as much as they learned. God was growing me through the use of my hands."

Chuck, on the other hand, had social justice as a strong suit from early on. As president of the black student organization at his college, he had an afro that made it difficult to get through doorways. He did inner-city work with juvenile gangs. Later as a professional, he wrote and lectured on the topic of racism.

Yet as he got older, he realized that financial giving was a weak area for him. More specifically, he would call himself stingy in the area of financial stewardship: "When you grow up in the inner city, you have a tendency to hold onto everything you can." But as Chuck was confronted about this area of his life, he became increasingly convicted that he needed to become more faithful in his giving.

Interestingly, Bob was always strong in financial giving. They each needed to grow in different ways, and they each had different strengths—and in this case, opposite strengths and weaknesses.

We all have different ways that we need to move toward integration, as we aim to make and grow as disciples after the pattern of Jesus—someone with hands, head, and heart all brought together. When that happens, it's not like we simply increase in all three of those areas. Each area is actually strengthened and changed by the presence of the others. The head (knowledge) strengthens and informs the heart and the hands. Our actions of doing what God wants (the hands) strengthen our hearts and our heads. Our hearts, in turn, become the wellspring of God's love shaping the rest of our lives.

Like a chemical reaction, the overlap becomes greater as the parts themselves change. That's integration—simultaneous increasing in each area and greater overlapping across the three areas.

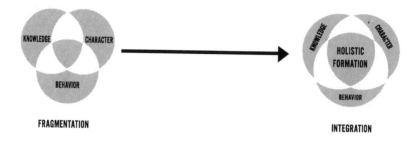

FRAGMENTATION

INTEGRATION

IF YOU CARE ABOUT THE RESEARCH...
A NOTE FROM CHUCK

The word "integration" originates from the Latin *integrātiō*, which means "renewal." To integrate is to combine various entities into a new, unified whole. As a result, the new entity is qualitatively different from the entities upon which the integration is based. The new entity also functions differently.

A relevant example of integration is found in calculus, a sub-discipline of mathematics. In calculus, an integral is the common area and summation of the relationship of variables in an equation. To determine what is common, mathematicians first must understand what is different among the various spate of functions. Applying these concepts to discipleship, we can ask: "What are the respective functions of the head, heart, and hands?" and "What is common among these entities when they are integrated?"

The head is the seat of knowledge and functions to process information and make decisions. The heart is the seat of character and functions to align decisions and behavior according to moral and spiritual principles. The hands are the seat of behavior and function to take action for effective living.

When the head, heart, and hands are truly integrated in the disciple, the integral is a transformed person—one who functions qualitatively differently than a person who is not transformed. The key word here is *functions*, as a new function is derived from transformation that is over and above the respective functions of the head, heart, and hands. The holistic disciple imitates Christ, and the function of this imitation is two-fold: to continually become more like Christ and to make more and better disciples. The apostle Paul is an example of a transformed person who imitated Christ.[12]

Our approach to discipleship typically is fragmented, not integrated. We need to move toward integration, but that's something that's not really possible with a one-size-fits-all approach to discipleship.

WHAT IS THE FRUIT OF A HOLISTIC DISCIPLE?

When we have integrated disciples who incorporate hands, head, and heart, we see they are vastly more likely to pass along that discipleship to others. Holistic disciples modeled on the pattern of Jesus multiply more disciples. They are fruitful. Consider Jesus' parable of the vine and the branches:

> Remain in me, as I also remain in you. No branch can bear fruit by itself; it must remain in the vine. Neither can you bear fruit unless you remain in me. I am the vine; you are the branches. If you remain in me and I in you, you will bear much fruit; apart from me you can do nothing. . . I chose you and appointed you that you may bear fruit—fruit that will last (John 15:4–5, 16).

Notice the mutuality described in this passage. Growth doesn't happen apart from meaningful connections with God and others. Fruitful disciples multiply both disciples and disciplemakers. We need to abide in Christ in order to bear fruit. We grow as disciples and make disciples at the same time. There's no waiting time, but a simultaneous influencing of the Spirit as we influence others. Our connection with the vine is clarified and evidenced by our fruit. Our fruit is only possible because of the vine.

> *Growth doesn't happen apart from meaningful connections with God and others. Fruitful disciples multiply both disciples and disciplemakers.*

The Great Commission also clarifies the intended result of our being disciples:

> Therefore go and make disciples of all nations, baptizing them in the name of the Father and of the Son and of the Holy Spirit, and teaching them to obey everything I have commanded you. And surely I am with you always, to the very end of the age (Matthew 28:19–20).

Being a disciple means you make disciples. It's part of the package. Biblically speaking, disciplemaking is not about perfecting believers but about actually making new followers of Jesus. Discipleship means both growing in our own discipleship and making other disciples. Every believer is called to do both, and they are two parts of the same whole.

The result of holistic discipleship is the multiplication of more disciples who are also holistic—which again, means being integrated in terms of hands, head, and heart. Those holistic disciples are also disciplemakers, who go on to make other holistic disciples, who make other holistic disciples. It's a never-ending cycle.

However, many people miss the core mission of Jesus: the need to multiply disciples. Unless we intentionalize disciplemaking and think about it from the beginning, we often miss it. It's not automatic.

Ongoing disciplemaking completes the bigger picture of the mosaic: when all the pieces of our various journeys of discipleship come together to create a picture of multiplying disciples and multiplying disciplemakers. That's how we know our discipleship process is truly working.

Rob decided to throw out the old discipleship curriculum—the kind where one section builds on the previous section so that you have to follow it all the way through in a linear fashion for it to make sense. The old curriculum was also designed to be processed via group discussion, meaning everyone would need to progress through the material together and at the same pace.

Certain phrases kept looping through his mind for the rest of that week: not linear but mosaic, listening to the Holy Spirit. He would need some kind of relational process that would enable him to keep the direction of the discipleship both individualized and flexible.

"Now that we're not using the curriculum—or any curriculum, for that matter—where does that leave us?" wondered Rob. "This should be interesting. Oh well, spring is coming . . . Out with the old, in with the new. We'll see where this takes us."

CHAPTER 6

GROWING TOGETHER IN GROUPS

After Rob had finished explaining this new approach to his group of key leaders, he looked out to see blank stares. Then the questions started:

> *"If we throw out the educational curriculum we've been using, then what do we do? What does that even look like?"*
> *"How will we make sure we cover what we need to cover? That section on prayer is important, you know, and it really should come at the beginning."*
> *"How do we even know what area we're supposed to be focusing on?"*
> *"This seems kind of touchy-feely, new-agey, if you ask me."*
> *"Why can't we just have Bible classes?"*

The pushback had begun.

Rob called Jim. "I'm just figuring this out myself, which makes it a bit challenging to explain, and justify, to others at the same time. It feels like I'm hitting a wall of resistance and it's hard to figure out if they don't understand me or if it's that they just don't like the idea."

"I have two thoughts on that," said Jim. "First, you may not want to throw out all of your existing programming at once. . . unless you want a very short pastoral ministry." He laughed. "Not everyone is ready for that. Don't push people beyond where they can go. Bring in the new, but leave some of the old intact as well. Offer new options to those who are receptive, but don't tear down what people already have. Love them, care for them, keep doing what you're doing. But think through who you need to be reaching out to and challenging."

"Second," he continued, "People may understand this new approach a bit better if they experience it. It might help you as well. Why don't you try this next time you meet: Break people into groups of three. Then give one person in each group the floor for thirty minutes to talk about how they're experiencing God and what they're hearing from him. The other two people can't do anything except listen and ask clarifying questions. No suggestions, no 'I did it this way,' no leading questions, no shifting the spotlight to themselves. Just listen, and then take a bit of time at the end to pray for that person. Then it's the second person's turn, then the third person's turn. The whole exercise will take between an hour and half and two hours. That's your whole meeting time, I believe. But it will give them a taste of what you mean by listening to the Holy Spirit in the context of community."

Rob felt a bit skeptical. Would people be willing to talk about themselves for half an hour? He usually felt stupid and self-conscious after about ten minutes. However, he decided to give it a try. . . possibly amending the time-frame to 15 minutes per person at least this first time around.

Very little of importance happens outside of relationships. God designed his people to live in the context of relationships—with him, with the created world, and with other people. It should be no surprise, then, that discipleship is also designed to be pursued in the context of relationships.

Discipleship in isolation doesn't work. We need others to provide feedback and challenge. We need others to be sounding-boards for our processing. We need others to help us listen to God and to help us understand where he wants us to grow. We need others to help us find a strategy for growth that will work for us. We need others to help steer us back on the right track when we begin to veer off course, become disobedient, and miss the mark in our lives. Change occurs in the context of relationships—and Jesus himself modeled its importance. The fundamental nature of discipleship is relational.

Change occurs in the context of relationships.

In the last chapter, we discussed the mosaic approach to discipleship. Here, we'll drill down into some of the specific ways community can support a mosaic approach to discipleship and what that can look like.

TAKING A PAGE FROM HEBREWS

So how are we to go about doing this discipleship in the context of community? What does it look like? The writer of Hebrews gives us some specific guidance:

And let us consider how we may spur one another on toward love and good deeds, not giving up meeting together, as some are in the habit of doing, but encouraging one another—and all the more as you see the Day approaching (Hebrews 10:24-25).

Let's unpack this rich passage, as it has a great deal to say about how we are to disciple one another:

- "let us *consider. . .* " The word *consider* implies intentional thought about how to help another individual. We are to take our time, sit down and consider the best way to spur one another on, recognizing that it may look differently for different people.
- "how we may *spur one another on. . .* " This phrase speaks to the very nature of community. Community is designed so that we might spur one another on toward growth. The word *spur* implies both challenge and encouragement. Our growth happens in the context of community. We help one another on toward that growth.
- "toward *love and good deeds. . .* " And toward what end are we spurring one another on? Toward love and good deeds. Not just love, not just good deeds—both. Here we see the highlighting of both the internal and the external, the being and the doing. That's holistic discipleship.
- "*not giving up meeting together* as some are in the habit of doing. . . " Consistent meeting together speaks to the intentionality of the relationships. In any community of people, relationships can fade out if we're not careful. We need to be intentional about maintaining our discipleship community.

So what does all this mean? It means that as we meet together, we come alongside one another to listen, to ask questions, to encourage, to challenge.

ONE OR MANY?

When we say "discipling relationship," most of us picture the traditional one-on-one disciple-disciplee relationship. That's how most discipling relationships in the church have been structured in recent years: One person who is older and more mature in the faith guides someone along who is younger and less mature.

Although that's the most common way we structure discipling relationships today, it's by no means the only way to do so. In fact, this approach by itself is incomplete. Jesus most often discipled in group settings, and most people have had multiple influential figures throughout their lives of faith.

Everyone can be involved in the disciple-making process through groups and relationships. *And* there is still a place for one-on-one focused discipleship relationships. It's not one or the other, but both/and.

One-on-one relationships bring the benefits of intentionality and individual focus. Often it can be helpful to have one person orchestrate the process of discipleship and provide consistent follow-up. There is certainly a place for focused and individualized discipling relationship—just don't make the mistake of thinking that's all there is.

Holistic discipleship requires not just one person, but the whole body of Christ. One person alone cannot disciple effectively (unless that person is Jesus!). If we want to become holistic disciples, we need the whole body of Christ. The larger community of believers, with all its wealth of gifts and experiences and perspectives, needs to play a role. Remember the 360 assessment: Multiple members of our networks provide us with feedback to help us grow.

> *Holistic discipleship requires not just one person, but the whole body of Christ.*

We all have a contribution to make in discipling others. We all bring something unique to the table. Making disciples is not an advanced-track activity for the mature; it's something God calls us all to participate in. Consider an adult with a developmental delay. Can she serve as the main point-person in a discipling relationship? Probably not. Can she still have an impact and be a part of making disciples? Absolutely.

> *Making disciples is not an advanced-track activity for the mature; it's something God calls us all to participate in.*

God has called us all to be a part of the Great Commission. The question is what our particular role looks like. How can we best be a part of a supportive system? Think of a phrase commonly used by the Vineyard group: "Everybody gets to play." There's something to be said for that, isn't there?

METHODS THAT WORK

Methods come and go. The underlying principles are what really matters. As Alwyn Cosgrove said, "Methods there are many, principles but few, methods are often changing, principles never do," which comes originally from the Ralph Waldo Emerson quote: "As to methods there may be a million and then some, but principles are few. The man who grasps principles can successfully select his own methods. The man who tries methods, ignoring principles, is sure to have trouble."

So why talk about methods at all? Because they give us structures to hang our hats on. They show us what a principle can look like in real life. Principles alone are often hard to grasp hold of and understand unless we can see how they look in more concrete form.

You don't have to use any of the methods listed below. You are perfectly free to make up your own approach. However, these are a few different ways people have put mosaic-style discipleship into place. They are ways people have found to be flexible and intentional at the same time.

Life Transformation Groups Bible reading, accountability questions, and prayer for small groups of two to four people http://loganleadership.com/resources/free-resources/life-transformation-group-ltg/	**Spiritual Breathing** Exhaling = confession of sin Inhaling = taking in God's Word http://newlife.godresources.org/empowered/5-spiritual-breathing/#.VS_z9vnF98E
Renovare The six streams of faith coming together to provide a holistic discipleship experience https://www.renovare.org/	**T4T** Bible stories with discussion questions designed to be easily passed along http://t4tonline.org/
ViaCordis Discipleship questions to ask one another based on twelve life commitments http://loganleadership.com/resources/free-resources/viacordis-expressions-life-commitments/	**Design your own...**

Whatever type of method you use, make sure it's holistic, including the hands, head, and heart. Make sure it's reproducible—simple enough to easily pass on to others. And make sure it's adaptable to groups, allowing multiple individuals to provide input and feedback. Many of these approaches are easy enough to be leaderless as well, so that peer groups can make ready use of them.

COMMON CHALLENGES

Many predictable challenges arise as you try to do discipleship with only peer-led groups such as these. Here are some of the common issues:

Content with where they are. Sometimes people are simply content with where they are. This is most often the case with those who have been Christians for longer periods of time. Remember when Jesus asked a man who had been paralyzed for thirty-eight years, "Do you want to get well?" It's an important question, because not everyone who is sick wants to get well. Likewise, not everyone who is *in need* of growth and change is *open* to growth and change. Sometimes it just feels safer and more comfortable to stay where we are.

Inward focus. An inward focus is one of the more difficult issues in discipleship. So much of what Jesus has called us to do has an outward focus; yet many contemporary churches imply through their teaching that all it means to be a good Christian is to read your Bible and pray every day. Such an approach has artificially separated inward growth from outward growth and has also artificially separated evangelism from discipleship. Left to our own devices, it's easier to focus on ourselves than on others.

Not faithful to the process. Other times in peer-led groups, the intentions are good but the follow-through is what's lacking. People just don't follow through on what they need to do; as a result, the whole group loses momentum. It's like the seed in the parable of the sower, which starts out strong but then gets choked out by weeds.

Linear view of growth. For most people, growth as a disciple is not a straight-arrow shot from A to Z. Instead, they take steps forward, along with missteps, steps back, lapses, and sometimes relapses—metaphorically falling off the wagon. Disciple-makers need to have patience with the process of growth and respect for individual differences.

What to do about these roadblocks? Most of us will try the beating-our-head-against-the-wall approach. As you may guess by its name, this approach is not a helpful one. It basically consists of trying to convince people who disagree with us, for whatever reason, that they should change and do it our way instead. Sound familiar?

Let's move on and take a look instead at some alternate responses to peer-led groups facing these issues.

INVEST IN WHAT'S WORKING

In John 15, Jesus tells the parable of the vine and the branches:

> I am the true vine, and my Father is the gardener. He cuts off every branch in me that bears no fruit, while every branch that does bear fruit he prunes so that it will be even more fruitful. You are already clean because of the word I have spoken to you. Remain in me, as I also remain in you. No branch can bear fruit by itself; it must remain in the vine. Neither can you bear fruit unless you remain in me.
>
> I am the vine; you are the branches. If you remain in me and I in you, you will bear much fruit; apart from me you can do nothing. If you do not remain in me, you are like a branch that is thrown away and withers; such branches are picked up, thrown into the fire and burned. If you

remain in me and my words remain in you, ask whatever you wish, and it will be done for you. This is to my Father's glory, that you bear much fruit, showing yourselves to be my disciples (John 15:1–8).

What does Jesus do with the branches that are not helping bear fruit? He cuts them off and throws them away. This practice in horticulture is called pruning. It allows the limited nutrients of the tree to go where they will be most productive. Essentially, instead of wasting its energy trying to make a non-productive branch bear fruit, the tree directs its energy toward those branches that are already productive.

What if we were to do the same in our churches? Although we may not (literally or figuratively) cut someone off, we may choose to direct our energy where it will make the most difference. So we can focus on those who are most receptive. We can invest our energy there, in those who are willing to be faithful to the process. When we see fruit, that's not our signal to look elsewhere because this branch is fine—that's our signal to provide an even more intentional investment.

We are to invest in what is growing: the fruitful and the faithful.

SHAPING DISCIPLES IN REAL-LIFE ENVIRONMENTS

Jesus used the world as his workshop for making disciples. He brought his disciples outside, into the real world, and gave them practical, hands-on experience. He didn't do a seminar on casting out demons; he had his disciples try it and then helped them figure out how to get it right. We learn how to swim in the same way—in a pool, not in a classroom. Although classes in swimming technique can be supplemental and helpful, there's no substitute for getting in the water and trying it.

Our character is shaped by facing real-life challenges that move us outside of our comfort zones. It's a little (or a lot) intimidating at first, but it's the only way to really learn.

Jesus sent us into the world, just as he was sent into the world (John 17:15–18). He had this very natural way of connecting with different people across the whole human spectrum: religious people, non-religious people, open, closed, rich, poor, male, female.

Jesus engaged with people and went where they already were. He sometimes went to those places the religious leaders of his day didn't go, the places where they were worried about being contaminated and made unclean. By the same token, when we encourage our people to go out and engage in real-life settings with all kinds of people, we help them develop real-life skills that they will need. We also help them look outward and develop hearts of compassion for those around them.

PROVIDE STRUCTURE. . . AND BE READY FOR A MESS ANYWAY

Sometimes people simply need some structure to keep growing in the right direction. Think of a tomato stake. The plant needs the structure of the stake to grow. That stake tells it it's growing in the right direction and provides necessary support.

Consider how you can provide a support structure for people who are in danger of losing their moorings or sense of direction. What might help them stay on track? Even doing something simple like having regular appointments, or having them know that you're going to ask them what they've done since the last meeting, can make a huge difference.

If we really engage in discipleship relationships consistently, it will make a difference. The results may be exciting and messy, but we will see God at work when we use an intentional, yet relational, process that is tailored to the needs and pace of the individual disciple.

> *We will see God at work when we use an intentional, yet relational, process that is tailored to the needs and pace of the individual disciple.*

We will see growth the same way we see children grow—in fits and starts, unevenly and not always at the times we expect it. Consider some of the similarities between parenting and discipleship: We provide some guidelines: "These are our basic expectations for all of our children." We provide relationships: "We will be with you to help you along the way." Then we leave room for the individuality of each child to blossom. In this way, they all become the unique individuals God has created them to be. As any parent knows, it's best not to say, "Why can't you be more like your brother?" None of us are *supposed* to be more like our brother.

During the growth process, we expect disciples, like children, to gradually take on more responsibility for themselves. We may spoon-feed a five-month-old, but hopefully we will not have to spoon-feed our five-year-old; in fact, a healthy older baby will soon start grabbing the spoon and trying to use it herself. As any parent can attest, growing toward maturity and compe-tence is a messy business. They don't always do it right the first time.

> *Growing toward maturity and competence is a messy business.*

In the same way, we should not continue to spoon-feed new disciples but encourage them to learn to feed themselves and take responsibility for their own growth. They will need to learn to listen to the Holy Spirit for themselves. They will need to reach out to their own families and friends to share what God has done for them. Will they make mistakes? Yes. But if we try to do too much for them, robbing them of the opportunities for becoming responsible for themselves, we will inhibit their natural development. The baby who is never allowed to hold the spoon will not be able to learn to use it.

Paul gives instruction about this principle in Galatians 6:1–5. He tells mature believers to help weaker believers to get on the right path. They should share in the burdens of weaker believers. However, the goal is for weaker believers to develop maturity and self-responsibility: "For we are each responsible for our own conduct" (v. 5, NLT).

Within a context of supportive community, we all can help one another grow toward maturity, spurring one another on toward love and good deeds.

The following Tuesday morning, Rob stepped into the coffee shop with a fresh-smelling spring breeze trailing him. He looked over to see Jim. "You know, I think God brought you here to this Midwestern town not for your grandchildren, but for a different reason—to help me! That listening exercise you gave me was dynamite!"

"What happened?"

"It's like lightbulbs were going on all over the room about what it means to listen to the Holy Spirit—and what it means to listen to others, as a matter of fact. You wouldn't think that something as simple as just listening to someone else would have much of an impact—especially when you're not allowed to give advice. But that was actually the beauty of it."

"Sounds like it gave you a clearer idea of how to proceed as well," observed Jim.

"Yes! These groups of three—triads, I'm calling them—are going to form the basis of our discipling relationships. We had fifteen people there this time. The group has been growing since we've been having these discussions on what it means to be a disciple. People are curious, even if they don't always agree. So we're going to start with five discipleship triads."

"You sound really excited," observed Jim. "Where do you see things going so far?"

"Well, it's still really early yet, but I feel like the most strategic place to focus is on getting people out from behind the church walls and into the world—not on my agenda but on theirs. I'm not sure what it will look like for them. In fact, I have an exercise in mind to help

them hear from God. . . Want to come along with me to the next gathering of all the triads?"

A couple of weeks later, Rob and Jim were walking toward the church in the early summer sunlight. The plan was for the gathering to begin inside the church building and end outside of it.

They were conducting their regular triad meetings, but Rob had asked them to add an emphasis on brainstorming and discussing ideas for increasing their outward focus. Each triad met together in different parts of the classroom. One was now a group of four, since a new person had been invited along. Rob and Jim walked around the room, listening in on what the people were talking about.

Caroline, the music teacher at college, would be working with some bands this summer over break—in some cases, with musicians who were her students during the school year—and she's been engaging with some of them in conversations about the connection between music and spirituality. Stan, one of the long-time small group leaders, had mobilized his group to look in on some of the elderly in their neighborhood who don't have families nearby. Burt has been talking about Jesus at various car meets. Gracie, Burt's wife, was telling her triad about trying to use her hospitality gift to invite over some of the antique-car guys and their wives. Laurel was talking about her plans for a summer camping trip for teen girls.

Toward the end of the triad time, Jim and Rob stood in the doorway of the room talking. Rob was concerned about one of the triads. One person seemed to be dominating that conversation because he had a lot of personal problems. "It's not like today is unique either," said Rob. "This guy always has a lot of personal problems. I'm afraid he's going to sink this triad."

"Yes, he may," considered Jim. "It sounds like he's someone who needs more individual care than a triad is designed to provide. Maybe pastoral care or counseling of some sort would be helpful. Maybe you could talk with him to determine whether you have the skill and expertise to help him, or whether he needs a trained counselor."

IF YOU CARE ABOUT THE RESEARCH...
A NOTE FROM CHUCK

At what point do we place the interests of the community over the interests of high needs individuals? In every community, there are people who require special attention. Some tax the community, sapping an exorbitant amount of time and effort. An ongoing concern about serving the interest of each individual must be balanced with serving the interest of the entire community. At stake is the community's overall health.[13]

"I'll do that. That does seem like it would be more helpful to him than the triad. I could see that the other two people today have no idea how to respond to him or what to do."

"That one situation aside, you know what I'm noticing here?" asked Jim. "I'm seeing that people are spending only about twenty-five percent of their time on what we normally think of as 'discipleship content,' and about seventy-five percent on life application. In most classroom discipleship approaches, it's the other way around."

"Do you think that's okay? I certainly don't want to give short shrift to Scripture," asked Rob, concerned.

"I do, actually," replied Jim. "Think of it this way. What's better? Someone who knows just the basics but practices most of it, or someone who knows a whole lot but only practices a little of it?"

Rob nodded in understanding. "Good point. I see what you mean."

"From my experience," continued Jim, "It's when people are actively making disciples and seeking to reach out to others that they grow the most on their own journey. Ideally, everyone should be simultaneously discipling as well as being discipled. That way they can look through the eyes of one person to see not only them, but also all the multiple generations that will follow them."

When the triads finished their discussions, they moved outside to pray. Instead of facing inward in a circle, they faced outward in a circle, praying for the world around them.

CHAPTER 7

DYNAMICS OF A DISCIPLING RELATIONSHIP

The triads had been running for a couple of months now, and summer was in full swing. Rob was in regular contact with the people who were a part of the triads. When he and Jim met for coffee next, Jim asked a very simple question, "How's it going?"

Rob reflected for a few minutes before answering. "Well, I guess overall I'm feeling encouraged. We're definitely making much more progress with triads where everyone can work on areas where God is leading them. It's certainly working better than the classes and I can sense that people have much more ownership over their own growth."

"But?" asked Jim, sensing Rob's hesitation.

"Well, some of the triads have exciting things going on. They're outreach-oriented, thinking through next steps for service and relational engagement with people who don't know Jesus. But most of the groups are having a hard time with the outward-focus piece.

They can do the inward focus—what we usually think of as spiritual growth. But they don't have an outward focus. I'm not sure what to do about that."

Rob ran his fingers through his hair. "How do I get the rest of the triads engaged in service and developing relationships with people who don't know Jesus? Some of them seem willing, but don't seem to know how. What do they actually do to reach out? What will that look like for them? Others seem hesitant or even a bit resistant. I think they're afraid of the outward focus."

"Do you see any patterns as far as which people are in which triads? Who's having a hard time reaching out?" asked Jim.

"That's just the thing," responded Rob. "It's the opposite of what I would have expected. The people who won't reach out are the ones I would have considered more mature in the faith, those who have been Christians for a long time and are really involved in the church. Jack and Elsa, for instance. They've been running our Sunday school program for years, but they won't talk to their neighbors. What's up with that?" asked Rob in frustration.

"Some people do have more difficulty reaching out than others. It can feel like too big of a leap. In those cases, you can give them baby steps. . . incremental, smaller actions that they can build on. One guy I started with couldn't conceive of talking about spiritual things with people who weren't already followers of Jesus. So we started with helping him talk with people about regular daily topics just to build some relational connection. That was the starting point for him."

"You wouldn't expect it," Jim continued, "but sometimes those we think of as the most 'mature' Christians do the worst with being outwardly focused. They often don't see the need for change, and many are used to taking an intellectual approach to Christianity rather than an action-oriented one. Sometimes they're less willing to be transparent about their failings too. I've noticed that peer-led discipleship groups often work better with new believers or seekers than they do with mature Christians."

Rob thought about that for a while. "Hmm. Maybe we need a new definition of 'mature Christians' if that's the state of things."

"Maybe we do." Jim looked out the window for a few moments before continuing. "Now, it is possible they just haven't gotten the hang of it yet. But this situation does remind me of a group I worked with one time. In that case, the wall I was hitting was a simple case of passive resistance. They were afraid of change; they were afraid of being made to feel uncomfortable; they were afraid of finding out that they weren't such good disciples as they thought they were. So they were subtly trying to block the initiative by 'not getting it.'"

"What happened?" asked Rob.

"I tried to explain it for a long time—longer than I should have, in retrospect. But eventually I realized that no matter how well I explained it or what good reasons I came up with, nothing was going to click. So I gave up."

"You just gave up?" Rob was surprised.

"There's a scriptural precedent for that, actually," laughed Jim. "Think about John 15—the pruning of the branches, where Jesus talked about investing our energy in what's working and not investing it in what isn't working. You see the same principle at work in Matthew 13—the parable of the good soil. The seed that fell on the good soil produced thirty, sixty, and one hundred times what was sown. That's where you want to focus your planting efforts," said Jim, tapping the table where he was indicating the good soil.

"Hmm. I never really thought about it that way. I don't really want to exclude anyone."

"You don't have to," Jim said. "You can keep all the other things in place—sometimes not doing that can spell doom for pastoral leadership. But by focusing more energy on people who are receptive, you're also more likely to get others on board. As success stories are told, it'll create motivation to have them experience this kind of dynamic life with God too. You can come back to revisit the invitation then and give them an opportunity to join you again.

"You're giving everyone a chance. Some people will choose to exclude themselves. There's actually no rule that says everyone in your church has to agree with you and be on board. They certainly weren't in Jesus' ministry, that's for sure," laughed Jim. "Find the people who are receptive and fruitful and invest your energy there. Maybe some of the others will come along in time. Maybe not. But it's like Henry Blackaby says in his book Experiencing God, 'Look for where God is at work, and join him there.'"

"That does sound really exciting," agreed Rob. "If I do that—invest in those who are receptive and fruitful—I think they'll need more than the triads. I think they'll need more individualized and focused development."

"What are you thinking of so far?" asked Jim.

"I'm not really sure. After throwing out my traditional one-on-one discipleship curriculum and then moving toward an outward focus, I'm kind of at a loss about what to do for the intentional development of individuals, especially since I know I personally can't be all things to all people. It takes the whole body of Christ to disciple a person."

"Well," ventured Jim. "Let's start by thinking through the purpose of a discipling relationship. If it's not just an end in itself, what is it? What is it designed to do?"

"I suppose you could call it a relational context in which broader development takes place—the place you learn skills, get sharpened, and think through what God has for you next," said Rob.

"Agreed," said Jim. "Then if that's the case, what qualities does a discipling relationship need to have in order to serve its purpose?"

Rob thought for a while. "That's a good question. I don't really have an answer, though. Let's try to process that through together."

Yes, let's process that through together: What *does* a discipling relationship look like? What is its purpose? What qualities does it need in order to fulfill that purpose?

Not just any relationship is a discipling relationship. A discipling relationship is a specific subset of relationships. It is the context in which disciples are made and developed. It is specifically geared toward facilitating growth and developing the kind of people Jesus talked about in the Great Commission—disciples who make disciples who make disciples. Given that purpose, here are four defining features of a discipling relationship:

- Intentional
- Developmental
- Supportive
- Focused

Let's look at each of these features in turn.

INTENTIONAL

A discipling relationship is a relationship with a purpose. It's not just casual—it's a relationship headed toward a goal. It's on-purpose, intentional.

Many people in contemporary churches talk about "doing life together." This aspiration is laudable and we'll address the important role of community in a later chapter. But how doing life together actually plays out is often quite different.

People enjoy one another and get together for a meal; good spiritual conversations are had. Everyone expresses the desire to do life together in an organic, non-linear way, which sounds wonderful. Then life gets in the way and they don't see each other for a while. Doing life together quickly dissolves into nothingness or just day-to-day life without intentional time set aside for reflection and relationship. Whenever there is some growth for one person, they're not able to capitalize on it in their discipling relationship because there is no regular, consistent time of connection. Trying to do discipleship haphazardly on the fly doesn't work.

A discipling relationship is an on-purpose relationship. It must be intentional and regular if it is to work. Think about it this way: What type of results would you expect for your children if you just sent them to school once in a while—when you and they felt like it, or when you could squeeze it in when rather than regularly and consistently?

> *A discipling relationship is an on-purpose relationship. It must be intentional and regular if it is to work.*

Long-term growth requires us to be there consistently in order to get the job done. Just dropping in every now and then isn't enough.

An important piece of success is simply consistency: to be intentional in your discipling relationship. Meet every week, or at least every month. At the end of each meeting, figure out specific next steps: "This week I'm going to. . . " Then when you get together next time, ask about those next steps. It's that simple.

DEVELOPMENTAL

A good discipling relationship is developmental. It takes people wherever they are and helps them move one step further. We are to give people assignments—or better yet, help them to identify their own assignments—that are appropriate to their developmental level and which will help them to learn from experience. Opportunities come up, so let people try them and see.

Jesus used this approach with his disciples: Try casting out the demon; try stepping out of the boat. He'd then debrief the experience with them to help them learn from it. In this way, Jesus would stretch them as they were able, while still providing support.

The people we are discipling often need support at the same time as they need to stretch. This concept can be described as "rubber bands" (stretch) and "shoelaces" (support). With rubber bands, no stretch equals no growth. But if you stretch people too far they break. And then there are shoelaces: Shoelaces need to be tied together to function well, just as people need to be tied together in relational networks in order to function well.

Optimal conditions for a discipling relationship include both an environment of emotional safety and appropriate amount of challenge. That balance can feel hard to strike at times, but both are important. Prayer and discernment are essential for determining the right amount of connection and the right amount of stretch.

As people grow and hit developmental milestones, affirmation is essential. Affirmation is the foundation of change. When people take on a new challenge, try to provide them with a lot of positive feedback for what they have done well. So often we pull out the grocery list of all the things that need fixing rather than focusing on the affirmations. That ties most of us up in knots inside. The more criticism we hear, the less energy we have to improve. Aim for a ratio of ten affirmations to every one correction.

Bob learned this lesson by experiencing it. When he was in seminary, a long, long time ago, preaching classes were a painful experience. The worst part was when he had to go to the preaching lab to be videotaped as he struggled to deliver a message. Having to listen to himself on tape seemed bad enough, but having to see himself too was just too much. He was truly terrible. Here is how Bob described that experience:

My school had some video technicians who would occasionally find a prospective preacher's bad habits or mannerisms and zoom the cameras in on them. When my hands imitated "spiders doing pushups on a mirror," they filled the screen with my hands. If these guys ever decided to produce a film called *What Not to Do When Preaching*, you can just imagine all the raw footage I gave them to work with.

Zooming in on those negatives seemed to make my preaching worse rather than better. I put more and more pressure on myself after viewing those painfully honest videotapes of my blunders. I was in a downward spiral.

One day, after resisting the temptation to take a sick day, I dragged myself into the lab and there was a new technician there. As we watched the videotapes together, Randy would make a comment from time to time: "Nice use of words there." "Good transition." He commented on the positives. Sometimes he had long pauses between those comments, but he only said good things.

At the end of the segment, Randy shut off the recorder and said, "Bob, let me share with you your three greatest strengths in speaking," and he went on to list them. When he finished, Randy made one more comment that transformed my communication ability and my confidence: "You don't get better by focusing on your weaknesses. You get better by accentuating your strengths."

During the one meeting Bob had with Randy, he noticed that Randy spent about ninety percent of his time on affirmation and reinforcing strengths. Randy had only one concrete suggestion for improvement, which was very doable. That session was a breakthrough for Bob. He had been so focused on what he was doing wrong that he was expending all of his energy trying not to make mistakes—and consequently, getting progressively worse.

It was freeing for Bob to experience this environment of affirmation, and it allowed him to address problem issues one by one. His preaching skills improved dramatically as a result.

Don't underestimate the value of helping people grow by focusing on what they do well. Positive reinforcement can work wonders as you disciple people.

**IF YOU CARE ABOUT THE RESEARCH...
A NOTE FROM CHUCK**

Unknowingly, perhaps, Randy had employed what is called "differential reinforcement of alternative behavior" (DRA). The technique increases the frequency of positive behaviors, while decreasing the frequency of negative behaviors. As Bob responded favorably to Randy's affirmation and reinforcement, he had less time and opportunity to make spider-like movements with his hands and engage in other distracting behaviors. The scientific premise underlying DRA is that desirable and undesirable behaviors cannot coexist simultaneously. Therefore, by increasing desirable behaviors (such as effective preaching skills), you automatically decrease undesirable behaviors (such as spider-like hand movements).[14]

SUPPORTIVE

As we talk about being intentional and being focused, let's not lose sight of the fact that we're also talking about a relationship. We're not just engaging in strategic planning; we're coming alongside like Barnabas and cheering people on. We're walking with them. They're seeing our faith in our life and there's a sense of encouragement. It's a real relationship.

How do we talk with them about what they're learning and experiencing? When people fall down, we help pick them up and dust them off. "Wow. That must have hurt. Are you okay? What did you learn?" When people experience a success, we celebrate with them and ask what can be learned from the experience.

> For you know that we dealt with each of you as a father deals with his own children, encouraging, comforting and urging you to live lives worthy of God, who calls you into his kingdom and glory (1 Thessalonians 2:11–12).

- We encourage: Yes, you can!
- We comfort: Yes, you will!
- We urge: Yes, you must! [15]

When people experience failure, we embrace their pain and help them to fail forward: "Carry each other's burdens, and in this way you will fulfill the law of Christ" (Galatians 6:2). We encourage, we comfort, we urge one another toward living lives worthy of God. That's the essence of how we help one another grow. We also walk with people through periods of uncertainty, loss, and grief—not with superficial platitudes, but with genuine heartfelt concern. We are there for both the good times and the difficult times.

FOCUSED

A discipling relationship is also focused: There is clarity about where you're trying to go and what you're trying to produce. As you disciple others, you have an end in mind. You help them reflect on where they are now in light of where they want to go.

In addition to having clear goals, part of being focused also involves accountability for those goals. In a discipling relationship, we not only help people set clear goals, but we walk with them as they accomplish those goals. We hold them account-able for their development, just as others hold us accountable for our development. That's part of maturity.

A discipling relationship is not simply membership or participa-tion in a church or organized faith community. It's not a superfi-cial, casual acquaintance. Rather, it's focused on clear, practical goals. A clear goal provides focus to a discipling relationship. Be sure it's not just vague; be specific.

Unclear or vague goals	Clear goals
I hope to grow in serving others.	Since I have identified hospi-tality as a possible spiritual gift I may possess, I will try three ways of expressing hospitality by the end of this month and will journal about my experi-ences and observations.
I want to spend more time with God.	I will set aside fifteen minutes on weekday mornings and thirty minutes on weekend afternoons to spend exploring different types of prayer.

One common mistake is to think that the type of maturity and participation described in the left column above equates to membership. It does not. In actuality, we can be in a church or organized faith community and still not be in a discipling rela-tionship. The distinction is simple: Our membership or partic-ipation itself does not mean we are focused on clear goals, or held accountable for those goals. A healthy discipling relation-ship does.

The air was still heavy with summer, but Rob and Jim were already seeing "back-to-school sale" signs as they took a walk around town. In spite of the signs, Rob wasn't feeling the kind of energy and anticipation he usually associated with the back-to-school season. Rather, he was feeling a bit stuck.

"What's wrong?" asked Jim.

"I've been thinking of the point you made about intentional development—investing in the disciples who demonstrate more fruitfulness. To provide more individualized attention, we need to create some one-on-one opportunities. To do that, I need to not only develop disciples, but disciplers too. The problem is, I've tried doing this several times before and I have failed pretty miserably. The most I've accomplished is to confer official status on people who were already doing it effectively."

"What have you tried so far?"

"Classes, books, me discipling them. . . It feels like I've tried everything! The problem is that none of the approaches actually teach people what to do in a discipling relationship. I've had people come up to me afterward and ask, 'Yes, the theory is all well and good, but what do we actually do when we sit down to disciple someone?' So they end up just reading through books together, which—as we've already established—falls pretty far short of effective discipleship."

Rob looked down at the sidewalk, his shoulders slumping. They walked in silence for a few minutes. Then Jim asked, "Can I tell you a story?"

"I was hoping you might have one," smiled Rob.

CHAPTER 8

OBEDIENCE AS THE CRUX OF DISCIPLESHIP

*"Carlos was a missionary serving among the poor in Mexico City,"
began Jim. "He wanted to invest in some discipling relationships,
but was struggling to find the time to do so, partly because most of
the people he was serving were already working long hours just to
support their families.*

*"One man Carlos wanted to disciple was Hugo. Hugo had a bakery.
He would get up at 3:00 am to do the baking, then he did the deliveries, then he sold from his shop. Usually Hugo wouldn't get home until
7:00 pm. He worked all day, leaving no time for additional discipleship studies.*

*"Carlos was discussing this dilemma with his coach, and his coach
asked him, 'Why don't you be like Jethro? Jethro went with Moses to
work, watched what he did, helped out, and spoke into Moses' life.
What would it look like for you to go to this man's place of business
and disciple him in the context of his life?'*

"A light went on for Carlos. He'd been thinking of discipleship as a time set aside where people came to him and they went through Scripture passages together. The idea of going to them and being with them in the course of their daily life opened up all kinds of new possibilities. Suddenly he had all the time in the world to invest in discipleship—and the Scripture passages could be lived out as they went along.

"When Carlos began showing up at Hugo's bakery, he helped out and the work started going faster. Sometimes they had time for more focused conversations while the bread was baking. Other times they went on deliveries together and looked for opportunities to engage in spiritual conversations with those bread-buyers who showed openness. Eventually, Hugo began asking Carlos questions about how he could run his business more efficiently, and Carlos was able to coach him through that process. It was a totally different paradigm for discipleship."

Jim had finished his story, and he and Rob walked on in silence for a while as Rob thought. "That's a totally different way to think about discipleship," he said eventually. "Discipleship isn't simply about reading a book together or going through a course of study. It's not an add-on to the rest of life. It is the rest of life—and how we can live it in obedience to God."

Discipleship isn't simply about reading a book together or going through a course of study. It's not an add-on to the rest of life. It is the rest of life—and how we can live it in obedience to God.

Peter, one of the original twelve disciples of Jesus, gives us a great example of the ups and downs of what it looks like to be a disciple in the course of ordinary life. Let's take this story as an example:

> Shortly before dawn Jesus went out to them, walking on the lake. When the disciples saw him walking on the lake, they were terrified. "It's a ghost," they said, and cried out in fear. But Jesus immediately said to them: "Take courage! It is I. Don't be afraid."
>
> "Lord, if it's you," Peter replied, "tell me to come to you on the water." "Come," he said. Then Peter got down out of the boat, walked on the water and came toward Jesus. But when he saw the wind, he was afraid and, beginning to sink, cried out, "Lord, save me!"
>
> Immediately Jesus reached out his hand and caught him. "You of little faith," he said, "why did you doubt?" And when they climbed into the boat, the wind died down. Then those who were in the boat worshiped him, saying, "Truly you are the Son of God" (Matthew 14:25–33).

What are some observations you can make from this story? Here are some of ours:

- Being a disciple means moving outside of your comfort zone.
- Unfamiliar circumstances are often scary, but we need to face our fears and respond by stepping into them (literally, in this case).

- Disciples need to make in-the-moment decisions about what faith and obedience look like in their immediate circumstance.
- Our steps of faith and obedience don't always go perfectly or as planned.
- God is with us anyway.
- We need others alongside us who will provide the encouragement to step out of the boat and the hand reaching out to catch us when we are falling.

The story of Peter stepping out of the boat is a great example of what discipleship looks like. What are we afraid of? What do we hear God calling us to do? How can we face the fears that may block us from taking action? Who do we have as a support if we fail?

What the specific fears and risks look like for each of us may be different. Where and how we need to be stretched varies from disciple to disciple, and we've already seen that as Bob and Chuck have discussed the very opposite ways they've been stretched. The common denominator is that we all have growth areas that require us to be stretched toward greater obedience, even in the face of fear. Facing our fears, stepping outside our comfort zones, doing what feels unnatural to us—all of these are central to discipleship. All the other tools and methods we use to disciple one another are used toward this end.

In this chapter, we will take a closer look at the way obedience functions as the central issue in the day-to-day life of our discipleship journey. We'll delve into specific tools we can use toward that end in the next chapter; but first, let's look at the defining features of obedience themselves.

LOVE AS THE MOTIVATION

"Obedience" can be a difficult word to hear. For many of us, it brings to mind legalism, checklists of rules, or even doing out of fear what someone else wants. The obedience God calls us to, however, is nothing of the kind. It has its roots deep in the love of God. We live in obedience to God out of response to his great love for us: "We love because he first loved us" (1 John 4:19).

True obedience of the heart, then, must have its motivation set firmly in the foundation of love. Consider how much easier it is to obey when we're coming from a perspective of love. A child who trusts and loves his parent will be willing to try something he's afraid of if that parent encourages him and provides support; picture, for example, a parent holding a boy's hand as he puts his toe into the water.

Likewise, we must have love as the motivation for our obedience if it is to be the kind of obedience God desires: "May he turn our hearts to him, to walk in obedience to him and keep the commands, decrees and laws he gave our ancestors" (1 Kings 8:58).

KNOWLEDGE IS FOUNDATIONAL TO OBEDIENCE

We are quite familiar with the first part of the Great Commission: "Go and make disciples." But the rest of Jesus' command includes this phrase: "teaching them to obey everything I have commanded you" (Matthew 28:19–20). If we are to be obedient to what Jesus has called us to do, we need to understand what obeying looks like. We need to learn the teachings of Jesus.

Knowledge is not an end in and of itself (that falls into the "all head" problem discussed earlier), but it is a necessary part of the whole. Knowledge of God and his Scriptures is what our life of obedience is based on. Some knowing is required for doing, just as some doing is required for truly knowing. The key is to act on what we do know, and to not let our knowing outpace our doing.

> *Some knowing is required for doing, just as some doing is required for truly knowing.*

Knowledge divorced from obedience was the Pharisees' core problem. "Knowledge puffs up while love builds up" (1 Corinthians 8:1). Knowledge was never intended to be an end in and of itself, but the foundation for a life of obedience. The challenge, then, is when our knowing—our learning—brings us face to face with something we're afraid of.

FACING OUR FEARS

"Fear not" is the oft-quoted greeting of an angel to a human. Biblical angels are not the cute little cupids we often depict; biblical angels are frightening. So "fear not" is a necessary greeting. It doesn't mean "don't feel afraid"—the angel expects that you already do feel quite afraid. It means "don't let your fear get in the way."

> *"Fear not" doesn't mean "don't feel afraid." It means "don't let your fear get in the way."*

When it comes to practicing loving obedience, self-awareness precedes action. We all have fears that can stand in the way of living as God wants us to live, and we need to acknowledge those fears to God.

Let's take one of the most common examples: Christians afraid to reach out to non-Christians. The fear there is often of rejection or awkwardness, and the consequence is usually avoidant behavior. Given the Great Commission, that's a pretty significant blockage to our discipleship. Because we are afraid, we avoid; and because we avoid, we become more afraid. It's a cyclical cause-and-effect relationship—one we need to interrupt. We miss major opportunities for making disciples because of anxiety. It's a pervasive problem, and the first step needs to be openly acknowledging our fears before God.

IF YOU CARE ABOUT THE RESEARCH...
A NOTE FROM CHUCK

Fear and anxiety can lead to paralyzing psychological conditions. While these emotions serve a God-given protective function—alerting us to danger and potential harm—when mismanaged they rob us of personal freedom, peace of mind, and the ability to live life to the fullest. Yet their crippling effects are among the most preventable and treatable emotional problems. We know a lot scientifically about their course of development, the conditions under which they persist, and the treatment steps necessary to overcome their crippling effects.[16]

MOVING INTO OUR DISCOMFORT ZONES

After facing our fears, the next step toward interrupting the cycle is moving into our areas of discomfort. After the recognition comes the action: We need to step into the places we normally wouldn't go on our own. That takes conviction.

Nehemiah is a good example of a godly leader who was terrified but stepped into his discomfort zone. He requested permission from the Persian king Artaxerxes to return to Jerusalem to rebuild the city. Nehemiah prayed to God and displayed the courage of conviction, even as he experienced terror and fear (Nehemiah 2:1–5).

As we disciple people, how can we help them take steps into areas where they're uncomfortable: reaching out to a new neighbor, sharing our story of faith, speaking up when we see someone being mistreated, and standing up for our convictions? Unless we first have taken similar steps, the answer is simple: We can't. Therefore, we must first step into our own discomfort zones.

If we have taken these steps, how can we help those we disciple to do so in ways that are productive? One way is by giving them assignments that are just a little beyond where they currently are. It is like the physical activity of resistance training. Our stamina and muscles become stronger as we gradually increase the demands we place on our bodies. Rising to that challenge will mean getting involved, gaining experience, and addressing fears.

Facing a challenge despite fear creates a sense of crisis—which is also the opportunity for growth. Typically, we avoid fearful situations and activities, when the real solution is to face the things we fear directly.

By putting someone in an awkward situation that's challenging for them (with some support in place, of course) we can help them overcome that fear. Let's say someone is afraid of dogs. His natural inclination is to avoid dogs. Instead, he can face that fear in a secure environment—say, being surrounded by harmless puppies for a week. People are physically and psychologically unable to stay at a high threshold of uninterrupted fear for a week. The fear lessens over time and he calms down.

When you're facing fear, it's like going into cold water: You can either jump in or wade in. Either way, when people move into their discomfort zones they often go on to do great and wonderful things.

One teenage girl was terrified of doing public speaking in any form. She was asked to do a Scripture reading at her church and, with great fear, she agreed. Some level of safety was ensured: The words were written down on the page so she wouldn't have to make up what she was saying and she wouldn't need to have anything memorized. After doing the reading and seeing it go smoothly, her fears lessened; she likely would feel more comfortable the next time she was asked to read.

Too often we allow our fear and anxiety to prevent us from stepping out in obedience or taking a risk. Instead of avoiding the pain, we can allow Jesus to get us through the pain. We must walk by faith, even though we're trembling. That's the framework for doing the things God calls us to that we would normally avoid.

**IF YOU CARE ABOUT THE RESEARCH...
A NOTE FROM CHUCK**

The technical term for the process being discussed in this chapter is "exposure." In order to grow, people need exposure to challenging situations in which they initially feel threatened. The human tendency is to avoid because of fear and anxiety. The solution is not to first try and get over your fear, but to face the challenging situation through prolonged and intense exposure. Although it seems paradoxical, our fear dissipates by facing what we are afraid of rather than by avoiding it.

Jesus expected his disciples then, and us now, to do things that take us out of our comfort zones—things we would not do if we were not disciples, and things that sometimes make no sense from a human perspective. The advantage for disciples is that we have the Holy Spirit who dwells in us as a Comforter, Jesus who guides us, the Word of God that gives us biblical principles, and disciplemakers who walk alongside us.[17]

A NON-NEGOTIABLE

What will the path of obedience look like for us? Like the rest of discipleship, it will look different for different people. We are not all called to the same things, and we all have unique ways we need to be stretched.

However, obedience itself is *always* a requirement. There is no exception clause for any of us who call ourselves followers of Jesus. Obedience in being a disciple, and in making disciples, is what God expects of us all. It is non-negotiable, for we are all being stretched and formed into the image of Christ.

We cannot pick and choose our path of discipleship. It is not only non-negotiable, but there are no substitutions. Just as King Saul made a burnt offering to the Lord *instead* of doing what the Lord had commanded him to do (1 Samuel 13), we also can make no substitutions. We cannot say, "You make disciples. . . I am a teacher only/an artist only/an encourager of the faithful only." What God has commanded *all* of us to do, as followers of Jesus, is to make disciples. We all do it differently, but we are all called to do it.

The kind of obedience we're talking about in this chapter—stretching, risking, stepping out of our comfort zones, taking action—is a kind of obedience that doesn't fit the paradigm of many Christians. Rather, many of us consider obedience to be avoiding things we shouldn't do, as opposed to doing things we *should* be doing. There's a big difference.

Rather, most of us consider obedience to be avoiding things we shouldn't do, as opposed to doing things we should be doing. There's a big difference.

THE NECESSITY OF COST

One important element of obedience is that there is always a cost. There is a cost to following Jesus, and that cost demands movement into areas where we will be uncomfortable. Consider the case of the rich young ruler:

> Just then a man came up to Jesus and asked, "Teacher, what good thing must I do to get eternal life?"
>
> "Why do you ask me about what is good?" Jesus replied. "There is only One who is good. If you want to enter life, keep the commandments."
>
> "Which ones?" he inquired.
>
> Jesus replied, "'You shall not murder, you shall not commit adultery, you shall not steal, you shall not give false testimony, honor your father and mother,' and 'love your neighbor as yourself.'"
>
> "All these I have kept," the young man said. "What do I still lack?"
>
> Jesus answered, "If you want to be perfect, go, sell your possessions and give to the poor, and you will have treasure in heaven. Then come, follow me."
>
> When the young man heard this, he went away sad, because he had great wealth (Matthew 19:16–22).

There is a cost to following Jesus. Is it a monumental monetary cost for everyone? Of course not. Not everyone has much money to begin with. But for this man, money was standing in the way of him and God, so Jesus called him to give it away. There is a cost for us all, because we all have something standing in the way between us and God.

> *There is a cost for us all, because we all have something standing in the way between us and God.*

Overall, the cost of discipleship varies from person to person. For Dietrich Bonhoeffer, the German theologian, it cost him his life at the hands of the Nazi regime. For Martin Luther, the leader of the Protestant Reformation, it cost him excommunication from the church and condemnation as an outlaw. For many Christians, the cost of discipleship might not be life-threatening, but it could cost them social isolation on the job, sacrificial giving, investment in hard-to-develop disciples, or flat-out commitment of time.

Chuck is currently stretching a young man in his men's group at church by encouraging him to deliberately behave differently from the other people in his place of employment and social gatherings. Many times in those settings, the men will engage in "guy talk" that is demeaning to women. The young man is understandably concerned about acceptance by his peers and wants to fit in, yet at the same time wants to pursue a lifestyle of excellence. Being obedient in this context requires something. There is a cost.

IF YOU CARE ABOUT THE RESEARCH...
A NOTE FROM CHUCK

One of the classics in Christian literature is Dietrich Bonhoeffer's *The Cost of Discipleship.* First published in 1937, Bonhoeffer distinguished between what he called cheap grace and costly grace. Cheap grace does not require repentance, church discipline, confession, discipleship, the cross, and Jesus Christ. On the other hand, costly grace requires following Jesus, a broken spirit and contrite heart, and submission to the yoke of Christ.

Bonhoeffer' own life was a testimony of costly grace. He was executed in a concentration camp by hanging—a punishment for his dissent from Nazism.[18]

A LIFELONG ENGAGEMENT

Obedience to Jesus lasts a lifetime. Unlike our careers and vocations, which eventually come to an end, there is no retirement clause for those of us who are disciplemakers. There are always new steps of obedience to be taken, and none of us ever truly arrives. At one stage of life, we might start small in overcoming our fear of, say, engaging with those who aren't following Jesus.

We could begin by engaging in small talk at social events like cookouts, baseball games, and PTA gatherings. From there, we could begin to form relationships and engage in conversations with more depth. For example, in a neighborhood book club, themes of meaning and purpose in life may readily come up depending on the novel being discussed. The key is being exposed to new and increasingly challenging situations, rather than avoiding those situations.

There is no retirement clause for those of us who are disciplemakers.

The kind of obedience Jesus commands requires all of us to step outside of some aspect of our lives that is comfortable and into a zone of discomfort. If we never come to a place of facing our fears, stepping outside of our comfort zones in Jesus' name, and start doing things that feel risky for us, then we never really fulfill the Great Commission. And that is the lifelong commission to which he has called us.

CONSEQUENCES OF OBEDIENCE

What we choose to do—whether we choose to live in loving obedience to God or not—matters. There are consequences to our choices, to ourselves, to those around us, and to the larger world. We must step out in courage if we are to make the kind of impact God is calling us to make.

What does Jesus have to say about those who are unwilling to act and risk?

> Again, it will be like a man going on a journey, who called his servants and entrusted his wealth to them. To one he gave five bags of gold, to another two bags, and to another one bag, each according to his ability. Then he went on his journey. The man who had received five bags of gold went at once and put his money to work and gained five bags more. So also, the one with two bags of gold gained two more. But the man who had received one bag went off, dug a hole in the ground and hid his master's money (Matthew 25:14-18).

If you know the end of the story, you know how displeased the master is with the servant who buried his money in the ground. The servant admits he was afraid, and so hid the money in the ground. The master had expected that the servant should do something with what he was given— invest it, or at the very least get interest on it. Inaction is not a substitute for obedience.

Inaction is not a substitute for obedience.

There are effects of obedience and effects of disobedience. What we do makes a difference. The Great Commission to go and make disciples isn't a suggestion or an option. It's a commandment. Yet many of the people who fill our churches don't consider it as such. After all, they are nice, upstanding, moral people. They aren't overtly hurting anyone. They give their tithes and offerings, are members of the worship and praise team, do not cheat on their spouses, and serve on the deacon board. But have they ever discipled anyone?

Not making disciples … is it categorically different from other forms of disobedience? Are we living as if it is?

**IF YOU CARE ABOUT THE RESEARCH…
A NOTE FROM CHUCK**

Jesus' spoken words, "Therefore go and make disciples of all nations, baptizing them in the name of the Father and of the Son and of the Holy Spirit, and teaching them to obey everything I have commanded you" (Matthew 28:19-20a) constitute an imperative. The entire process involves going, baptizing, and teaching to obey, but the only *imperative* verb is "make disciples." (The rest are participles.) In this, Jesus gives a clear, unequivocal order and direction.

As in many imperatives, the subject of the sentence (you) is implied but not explicitly stated. It is second-person-plural imperative. The implied subject of all of the verbs is "you"—all of the people who were listening, and by extension, us. The upshot is *"You* make disciples as you go." That's why failure to make disciples is also failure to be a fully developed growing disciple.

JESUS AS A MODEL OF OBEDIENCE

In Scripture, we see Jesus as a model of obedience to God the Father. Even coming incarnate to earth was an act of submission:

> In your relationships with one another, have the same mindset as Christ Jesus:
> Who, being in very nature God, did not consider equality with God something to be used to his own advantage; rather, he made himself nothing by taking the very nature of a servant, being made in human likeness. And being found in appearance as a man, he humbled himself by becoming obedient to death—even death on a cross! (Philippians 2:5–8)

In this passage we see humility and obedience, even unto death. Sometimes we think that because Jesus is divine, facing death came easily to him. Not so. We see his struggles in Gethsemane—that window of time when he could see what was coming and didn't want to endure the agony of doing it. He prayed that God would take the cup of suffering away from him if possible. Luke 22:44 describes his experience: "And being in anguish, he prayed more earnestly, and his sweat was like drops of blood falling to the ground." Yet even in the face of anguish and pain—and a very natural desire to avoid it—Jesus submitted his will to the Father's in humble and loving obedience.

Likewise, our obedience must flow out of love for God. He is there, holding our hand as we dip our toe into unfamiliar waters. Just as when Peter stepped out of the boat, Jesus is right there with us through the fear. And that is how we grow in faith and love.

Next time Rob came into the coffee shop, Jim wasn't there yet. While Jason, the barista, was making Rob's drink, they were making some small talk, as they had gotten to know each other over the months. Then Jason glanced up hesitantly at Rob and asked, "So you're a pastor, right?"

"Yeah."

"Well, this might sound weird. . . in fact, I'm sure it will sound weird. . . but my dog died yesterday. I love—loved—this dog. I had him for ten years, all the way through high school and college."

"I'm really sorry," said Rob. "I know how attached we can get to our pets. Sometimes it feels like they know us best."

"Yeah," agreed Jason. "Anyway, I'm having a really hard time with it and I was thinking it might help to do a funeral of sorts. I know that's weird. . ."

"Not at all," said Rob. "It's a real loss, and it's always helpful to grieve just like anything to which you are deeply attached. We can talk that through and then gather to say a few words ... formalizing the occasion, so to speak."

"Yes," agreed Jason, looking relieved that Rob didn't seem to think he was a nut case. "Thank you."

"I can come by tomorrow afternoon if you'd like."

"That would be great. Thanks again."

When Jim came in and they sat down, Rob told him about the con-

versation with Jason. "You know, something like this is an opportunity I never would have had if I hadn't been more intentional about taking the time to get to know people and build some relationships. I'm really grateful I did."

Jim smiled, and they turned the conversation back to where they had left off last time: facing fears.

"Okay," said Rob, "I think I get the idea of facing our fears and stepping into the unknown as part of our discipleship. I can see the different ways my leaders may need to be stretched and grow. Burt may need to become a bit more relationally vulnerable. That will be really hard for him. Caroline will need help with time management and strategic thinking. In some ways, those are simply skills, but I do think it will be spiritually stretching for her too. Others need to be nudged in different directions. And I think I intuitively know how to do that." Rob stopped, frowning out the window.

"But?" prompted Jim.

"But how do I teach them how to disciple others? How do I teach them how to stretch others? I can't think how to communicate that. Some of my leaders, like Stan for example, will just intuitively get it. I already see him doing some of these types of things. But how will I explain it to some of the others? I already know I'm going to get blank looks and then they'll ask, 'So what do we actually do?'"

CHAPTER 9

THE TOOLS FOR MAKING DISCIPLES

"Yes!" exclaimed Jim. "That's precisely the right question: So what do we actually do?"

"I guess I don't share your enthusiasm quite yet," responded Rob with eyebrows raised.

"I suppose the reason I get excited about this part is that with all of the concepts involved in discipleship, this part feels most manageable to me. I'm not saying it's easy, mind you. Just that there are clear, concrete skills that come into play here that can help us with stretching. We can all learn them, and they work. I suppose it appeals to the part of me that thought of being an engineer before becoming a missionary," smiled Jim. "So let's go through some of these specific tools that can be used to make disciples. Once you have the basic framework of obedience, it's time to get out the tools."

This is discipleship in the context of life. How different is this approach from the way we usually think of discipling relationships? Most of us think of set meetings, maybe once a week for an hour or two, in which two people work through a book or a study together. But real discipleship is much more than that. It takes place in the dining rooms, on the playgrounds, in the bakeries—anywhere. We are to disciple in the same way we are to teach our children:

These commandments that I give you today are to be on your hearts. Impress them on your children. Talk about them when you sit at home and when you walk along the road, when you lie down and when you get up. Tie them as symbols on your hands and bind them on your foreheads. Write them on the doorframes of your houses and on your gates (Deuteronomy 6:6–9).

This is discipleship in the context of life.

In addition to being biblical, there are numerous advantages to this kind of a discipleship approach:

- As you are discipling others, you're engaging yourself in their world, seeing what life is like through their eyes.
- You often find ways to be helpful, as Jethro was to Moses (Exodus 18).
- You view discipleship more as a way of life, not as an extra meeting.

In this chapter, we'll take a look inside the discipling relationship. What does it look like? What do we actually *do*? We'll walk through some specific methods, but never forget that it's a matter of discerning the Holy Spirit's leading as we determine what tool or combination of tools to use at what point. Discipling is more of an art than a science. As an art, it does not discount science. It simply uses scientific knowledge in an artful manner.

JESUS' CARPENTRY TRADE AS A METAPHOR FOR DISCIPLING

As we stated earlier, Jesus was a carpenter. He understood the process of taking raw materials and shaping them into something new and different. Jesus knew what he was looking for. Similarly, in obedience to the Great Commission, disciplemakers shape other disciples who become the kind of people God is looking for. Let's examine the carpentry metaphor in more detail.

First and foremost, good carpenters have vision. They begin the process of forming and fashioning with raw, unfinished materials. In its original form, the material may be unappealing; it might seem useless and/or of minimal worth. What good is a log from a dead tree? But good carpenters see what appears to be useless as something of worth, value, and potential. They do not simply see a dead log but an ornate table, a decorative door post, a sturdy chair.

Second, good carpenters are skillful. Jesus would have needed to be adept at taking the necessary steps to complete a project. Each step in building a product was a prelude to the next. The materials used in the process had to undergo stages of transformation—for transformation is a process. But without the proper skill set, transformation would be impossible.

Third, carpenters use a variety of tools: hammers, saws, and chisels, to name just a few. They have a toolkit to work from to form and fashion their products, and good carpenters know how to use their tools. Saws serve one purpose and screwdrivers another. Sometimes they use hammers, sometimes chisels. For master carpenters, the keys in using their tools effectively are purposefulness and timing.

Fourth, good carpenters specialize in uniqueness. In their paradigm, no two finished handmade products are ever exactly the same, even those that look very similar. This would mean that Jesus' forming and fashioning must have varied to some degree with each product. In his work, every finished product was unique.

Vision, skillset, toolkit, and valuing difference—collectively, these are the carpenter's trademarks. Here we take our cues from Jesus, the Rabbi and master carpenter of spiritual formation. As disciplemakers, we begin with unfinished and sometimes raw human material. We do not choose what people are like when we begin the process of discipling them. We begin where they are in their spiritual journey. But like good carpenters, we also begin with a good understanding of what they are to become. We then approach disciplemaking as a process, skillfully using our discipling tools, and shaping each disciple based on their individual differences.

Vision, skillset, toolkit, and valuing difference—collectively, these are the carpenter's trademarks.

Here are some tools we can use in our discipling relationships to help one another grow toward becoming holistic disciples of Jesus. The context is the discipling relationship, and the tools are what happen inside that relationship; the tools are what we do. The following tools in the discipleship toolkit are practical and biblical. They also are grounded in the social and behavioral sciences.

Bob's father always told him, "Use the proper tool for the job." Remember that a good discipler doesn't just use these tools randomly; there's a synergy and a method. There are times to use a hammer and times to use a screwdriver—and those are not the same times. Tools are to be used with the end product in mind, and at the same time answer the question, "What does this particular person need at this particular time?"

By learning how to use all the different tools, you can begin to use more discernment about when to use which one. We need to lean on God's wisdom to use the proper tool for the job. What are those discipleship methods?

Social modeling
Questioning
Scaffolding
Reframing
Shaping
Confrontation
Direct instruction

All of these discipleship methods function together with each other in a way that makes the whole work together.

With these strategies and techniques, we can give those we are discipling the right amount of challenge in the right way to support their growth. We'll need to take their individual differences into account, letting the Spirit lead as we select the proper tools for the specific job. In this way, we'll be able to move together as a community toward the right destination: Becoming disciples while making disciples who make disciples.

SOCIAL MODELING

In social modeling, people learn through observing and imitating others. This is the same way children learn: by watching what the adults around them are doing, and then imitating those behaviors. Parents understand this dynamic. One father watched as his three-year-old son played with a toy tool set. The boy began banging his plastic hammer, and then suddenly swore. Dad recognized immediately where that behavior had come from.

Social modeling can be used as a general tool for demonstrating how to live out our lives as disciples. The way we treat people, conduct our personal and work affairs, establish priorities, and spend our time—these set an example for others to follow.

However, social modeling can also be used as a specific tool for teaching a particular aspect of discipleship. Let's say someone you're discipling observes you engaging in a spiritual conversation at a cookout with some people who don't know Jesus. They can see you doing that in a way that feels natural and good, and so they now have a model to emulate.

Sharing the gospel with others, leading a small group, and lovingly confronting another Christian—these are examples of the many skill sets that can be modeled in forming disciples. Let's say someone we're discipling is fearful of sharing their faith with people who don't yet believe. Start small. Does that person have a dog? Do they walk that dog? Could they talk with other people who are out walking their dogs? Not about faith necessarily, just relationally? Sometimes baby steps are the place to start.

Just as children watch adults, disciples watch other disciples. Are you living out what you want other people to become? If someone were to follow you around for a whole week, what would they learn about the life of a disciple based on your behavior? Remember that our life of faith is motivated by the gospel of grace in the power of the Spirit—and on that foundation, we form the behavior of disciples.

Social modeling also can be used together with direct instruction. First, explain how something works (direct instruction), then model that behavior (social modeling). This approach is sometimes known as show-how training:

Show-how training

I do, you watch
I do, you help
You do, I help
You do, I watch
You do, someone else watches

Jesus lived alongside his disciples and did things together with them so they could observe. For example, the disciples didn't know how to pray and asked, "Show us how to pray." So Jesus taught them the Lord's Prayer as a model (Matthew 6:9–13).

Discipleship is the same now—we live alongside each other. Discipleship is not limited to the confines of a specific meeting time and place. Someone you're discipling will be watching how you live. Consider: What are you modeling? What are others seeing? Moreover, deliberately model the specific behaviors that you want the people you disciple to develop.

IF YOU CARE ABOUT THE RESEARCH...
A NOTE FROM CHUCK

Albert Bandura is the father of social learning theory. In a series of studies in the early 1960s, collectively known as the Bobo Doll Experiment, he investigated children's responses to the aggression of an adult model to a Bobo doll, an activity they observed. He concluded that learned behavior results from observing, imitating, and modeling. The effectiveness of modeling depends on learners having an imitative repertoire. They must be able to pay attention to the behavior of the model and also perform the demonstrated behavior.[19]

QUESTIONING

David spent much of the Psalms asking questions of God and reflecting. Jesus asked his disciples a lot of questions to help them process their ideas: "But who do *you* say that I am?" If you count the number of times Jesus asks questions in the gospel accounts, there's an incredible number. Why would he ask so many questions? To get people to look at themselves in relation to God and to create a place for reflection.

Questions help us reflect, examine ourselves, and learn. Many of the times we want to teach or instruct, we should be asking questions instead. Never tell someone something you can get them to think of for themselves. It should become second nature to ask questions of those we are discipling to help them think, engage in self-reflection, and take some responsibility for their own growth as a disciple.

Questions basically need to be integrated into all the other techniques. Although we have questions down here as a separate category, know that they're integrated into all the other categories. They are orchestrated together: We ask questions as we reframe; as we shape we also model: "What other options do you see?" "What are you afraid of?" "What are you observing as you watch me?"

As we develop authentic discipling relationships and trust is established, our questioning may become more pointed and personal: "In light of what you now understand about obedience to God, how are you realigning your priorities?" "What steps are you taking to overcome your bad habit?" "How can the people on your job tell that you're a disciple of Jesus?"

Learn to use these tools in combination. Don't just use the one approach you're most comfortable with, but use the most appropriate tool for the situation.

IF YOU CARE ABOUT THE RESEARCH...
A NOTE FROM CHUCK

As a teaching tool, questioning is as old as the human race. God questioned Adam and Eve to educate them about their sinful condition. In the dialogues of Plato, Socrates masterfully used questions to instruct and argue important issues.

Educational psychologist Paul Eggen states that effective questioning serves a number of purposes: stimulation of thinking, formation of relationships, reinforcement of basic skills, involvement of reticent learners, refocusing of attention, and enhancement of self-esteem. Additionally, effective questioning complements other learning tools.[20]

SCAFFOLDING

Consider the image of a scaffold around a building that is being constructed or restored. The scaffold is something temporary that you stand on while you're working on the permanent structure.

In discipleship, a scaffold provides a temporary foundation upon which to learn, grow, and develop. It's kind of like a walker for toddlers. The walker is not meant to be permanent, but to help develop walking skills so that they're guided toward independence. When they no longer need it, the walker goes away. We see this same concept in Scripture:

- In Hebrews 5:12-14, where the writer talks about progressing from milk to solid food: "In fact, though by this time you ought to be teachers, you need someone to teach you the elementary truths of God's word all over again. You need milk, not solid food! Anyone who lives on milk, being still an infant, is not acquainted with the teaching about righteousness. But solid food is for the mature, who by constant use have trained themselves to distinguish good from evil."
- In Galatians 6:1-2, where we are instructed to carry the burdens of weaker brothers and sisters that they might grow to carry their own eventually: "Brothers and sisters, if someone is caught in a sin, you who live by the Spirit should restore that person gently. But watch yourselves, or you also may be tempted. Carry each other's burdens, and in this way you will fulfill the law of Christ."

While Chuck was working on his master's degree, he led a Bible study in the graduate residence hall. Several members of the group weren't initially believers, but came to faith through the process. In some cases, Chuck needed to give them a lot of emotional support. One woman from an abusive family situation wasn't functioning at a high level. Chuck would meet with her and help her think through how to move forward. He served as scaffolding, as she emotionally and spiritually became more and more responsible.

The risk, of course, is creating unhealthy dependence or getting in over our heads trying to deal with issues we're not equipped to deal with. Chuck also had that experience. When he was in his early twenties and before he was far enough along in his training in counseling, he was discipling a young man who was suicidal. The relationship was emotionally draining, and eventually fell apart.

With scaffolding, we're there as a support—not just us individually, but our whole community. Often it takes more than one other person to help us carry our loads. In doing so we need to be strategic about not creating unhealthy dependence and making sure that others are able to increasingly do more themselves, as we gradually remove the scaffolds and they take steps toward greater maturity and independence. If we keep people dependent, that's not helping them. For example, if we and others are still giving the same level of support we were three years ago, that's not scaffolding but unhealthy dependence—and immaturity is not a fruitful outcome of discipling.

What does scaffolding look like in discipling relationships? It can be something as simple as using graphics and visuals to help people learn a concept. It can involve taking disciples to seminars, workshops, and conferences. It can involve introducing them to more mature believers who can undergird them with support. It can be coaching them as they take on their very first leadership position. It can involve asking someone to recount a time they heard from God, reminding them that that's what it feels like to hear from God, so that they grow increasingly able to hear from God for themselves. Eventually the scaffolding is no longer needed.

IF YOU CARE ABOUT THE RESEARCH...
A NOTE FROM CHUCK

Scaffolding is actually an umbrella tool that incorporates several strategies and benefits. As an instructional tool, scaffolding allows people to learn through what Vygotsky called the "zone of proximal development"— the difference between what a learner can do *without* help and what he or she can do *with* help. In this phase, learners benefit the most before they are able to independently perform tasks. The goal is to help people to eventually be able to do it on their own without help.[21]

REFRAMING

Reframing means helping people see things in a different way: through a new lens, from a new perspective, or with a different interpretation. Often when we look at a situation by ourselves, we can see only one possible interpretation: "The way that person is looking at me, they must dislike me." Yet with reframing, we can see many alternate interpretations: Maybe that person is thinking about a problem they're trying to solve; maybe they're having a bad day; maybe you remind them of someone else and they're reflecting on that relationship.

Reframing can help people see differently. Jesus did this many times in the Sermon on the Mount. There he used the construction, "You have heard X, but I tell you Y":

You have heard that it was said to the people long ago, "You shall not murder, and anyone who murders will be subject to judgment." But I tell you that anyone who is angry with a brother or sister will be subject to judgment (Matthew 5:21–22).

Jesus then does the same thing with adultery, divorce, oaths, revenge, and enemies. He is using reframing to help people see the deeper issues of the heart. Reframing helps the disciple look at something from a new angle—an angle they would not have considered without the use of this tool.

Reframing helps the disciple look at something from a new angle.

When we begin discipling people, they don't come to us as blank slates, but with all kinds of preconceived ideas, beliefs, and values—some that align with God's perspective and some that don't. Reframing can help them open up their perspective and consider the possibilities.

Bob uses reframing regularly when he coaches ministry leaders. For example, he had been working with a church planter whose plant had failed. What had looked like a great opportunity turned out not to be, and the planter was having a really hard time accepting that reality and moving on.

Bob reframed it as a loss, which it was. It was the loss of a long-held dream, and the planter was going through the stages of grief. "What you hoped for didn't happen and you need to grieve that loss. Of course it feels awkward to embrace what's next. What you're experiencing sounds quite normal to me."

Reframing often has the powerful effect of helping us see that we're not alone in what we're feeling, or in normalizing what we're going through. One ministry leader was recounting a lack of energy and passion for what he was doing, as well as increased difficulty in focusing. Bob, after listening for a while, asked the man to recount all the different projects he had going on, as well as all the major life changes he'd had in the last year. After the man had done so—and *heard* himself doing it—he sat back and exclaimed, "Wow, of *course* I'm exhausted and having trouble focusing." The issue wasn't self-discipline, as he had suspected—it was simply that he had too much on his plate to do well and it was wearing him out.

That's the power of reframing. Consider how Jesus used it in this story:
People were also bringing babies to Jesus for him to place his hands on them. When the disciples saw this, they rebuked them. But Jesus called the children to him and said, "Let the little children come to me, and do not hinder them, for the kingdom of God belongs to such as these. Truly I tell you, anyone who will not receive the kingdom of God like a little child will never enter it" (Luke 18:15–17).

**IF YOU CARE ABOUT THE RESEARCH...
A NOTE FROM CHUCK**

According to Thomas Sexton, reframing has three dimensions to it. The first is acknowledgement: We all come to the table with existing points of view about things. Before you can take in an alternate view, you need to be clear on what your existing view is. The second is reattribution: There is a different way to look at it than the way you're currently looking at it. This is not a liability but an asset; God may be using this different perspective to open new doors. The third is assessment: We take that new point of view and incorporate it into our thinking. In discipleship, we can use that dimension to help people change and behave differently. "Do not conform to the pattern of this world, but be transformed by the renewing of your mind" (Romans 12:2a).[22]

SHAPING

Shaping means using positive reinforcement to gradually change people's behavior. It means modifying behavior to become more refined, useful, and competent. This tool is like using a chisel to form and fashion a product. Through the appropriate use of reinforcement, we can shape people's behaviors to be more in line with Jesus' vision of discipleship. The shaping and changing of behavior takes place over time, as the prophet Isaiah described: "Yet you, Lord, are our Father. We are the clay, you are the potter; we are all the work of your hand" (Isaiah 64:8).

Take a disciple who is shy, typically avoids meaningful conversations with new people, and never speaks up in a group. He had a casual conversation with his neighbor. Celebrate that! At some point, they may touch on spiritual matters. Celebrate that! Progress, not perfection, is what matters. Celebrating progress will encourage people to move closer to the desired behavior.

Progress, not perfection, is what matters.

In using shaping to disciple people, we need to be sure not to wait until a person is living a behavior out perfectly before we affirm. We should even be affirming attempts or effort in the right direction. Just like cheering on a baby who is learning to walk, we encourage even failed attempts. As we celebrate people's efforts, they will try again and keep trying.

In using shaping, we start where people are and then gradually move them forward through encouragement and the highlighting of progress. Identify and affirm even small steps in the right direction. Small steps, not necessarily giant steps, are often what's needed.

Bob remembers a time he used shaping when he was pastoring. A high-school student was playing guitar on the worship team at church. This young man had his head down, focused on his instrument, with a look of intense concentration. His face was scowling and knotted up, as if he were trying to pass a kidney stone. He looked terrible.

Since Bob was the pastor and had to sit in the front row, he hardly worshipped for weeks as he tried to figure out what to do. He knew that in this case criticism would be destructive. Then one week, Bob noticed the young man smile. It was brief, but real. So Bob complimented the behavior and went out of his way to reinforce it.

At the next service, this young man kept popping his head up and smiling periodically. It was a bit distracting, but he was trying and Bob kept affirming him. Over time, that young man became a warm and inviting worship leader.

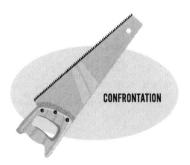

CONFRONTATION

If your first impulse is to go straight to confrontation, check that impulse. There are probably other things you would be better off doing instead. This particular tool should be used judiciously.

That said, there are times when someone truly needs to be challenged and nothing else will be very effective. Scriptural examples include Paul confronting Peter, Nathan confronting

David, and Jethro confronting Moses. Confrontation is especially needed when a pattern of behavior has been demonstrated. (In some cases, of course, there are one-time misbehaviors that require confrontation as well.) It can be used as an intervention when there's a pattern and when other tools haven't worked to effect change.

The essence of confrontation is pointing out inconsistencies. The inconsistencies can be between behavior and motive, behavior and what is said, or behavior that contradicts other behavior. You do this, but your attitude conveys something else. You say this, but you are doing that. Or, you are acting one way in this context and doing the opposite in another context. What's going on there? Doing X seems inconsistent with your values.

Bob remembers a time early on in his ministry when he was serving as an intern. A man helping in his discipleship confronted him. Bob had been running chronically late for meetings, and the man told him, "You're not late because you didn't run fast enough. You're late because you didn't start early enough. When you're late, you're communicating that you're the most important person in the room and that others can wait for you because you're that important."

Bob has never forgotten that, and he now makes an attempt to be early, which then allows margin for the unexpected—which frequently happens.

Be careful never to shame or to scold, even when it's a matter of sin or serious dysfunction. The goal is to help the person, not to assault them. There's no need for a missile blast when a simple conversation may take care of the matter.

Always start from the foundation of a trusting relationship, and approach it as a problem-solving issue not a blaming issue. Be sure to make any confrontation about actual behavior, not about personal character. Remember that the end-game in confrontation is healing, change, and spiritual transformation.

Sometimes people can feel bad, on either side of a confrontation, but the conversation itself needs to be on a higher plane. We must want the best for the other person, not to shame them or take them down a peg. If our own motives are wrong, we're not the right person to be doing this confrontation.

**IF YOU CARE ABOUT THE RESEARCH...
A NOTE FROM CHUCK**

Confrontation is a micro-skill designed for use in counseling and psychotherapy, although it has much broader application in improving human functioning. Allen Ivey, the originator of micro-skills, defined confrontation as a supportive challenge to help individuals examine themselves or their situations more fully and then resolve their difficulties.

Charles Ridley and Steven Goodwin later applied the skill to leaders in ministry. In the first phase of confrontation, critical examination, the purpose is to determine whether the behavior in question is a problem and needs to change. In the second phase, direct challenge, the purpose is to connect the problem behavior to its causes and consequences in order to help the person change.[24]

DIRECT INSTRUCTION

Direct instruction is the default for many of us in ministry, probably because it's what we're used to and it's often the easiest discipleship approach to take. We may feel better when engaging in direct instruction—it makes us feel as though we're actively doing something—but it doesn't necessarily result in changed lives on its own. Nevertheless, direct instruction has a place in the discipleship toolkit.

Direct instruction means the teaching of content. At first, it may sound as if direct instruction is the diametrical opposite of the kind of whole-life discipling we are talking about. But it's not the opposite; it's just one piece of the whole. Although people have tried to replace relationship with instruction in some contexts, there is a still a need for at least some instruction—probably just less than we think there should be!

So how can we stack the odds in our favor when we do need to use this tool? First, before we go to direct instruction, we should ask questions to draw out what people already know. Sometimes others find it demeaning when we tell them things they already know, just assuming they haven't heard or thought about it before.

Start from the top: "Tell me what you already know about topic X." From there, we can ask follow-up questions, summarize what we hear them saying, and unpack it. Only after that do we start dispensing wisdom. But even then, when we see a light bulb come on, sometimes it's best not to finish the lecture, but see how much further they can take it based on what's in their own minds. In this way, we can help others do as much of the thinking as possible, just filling in the gaps that require further illumination.

We should also try to integrate direct instruction with experience as much as we are able. After people have had some ministry experience, they are much better able to grasp direct instruction. They then have better handles and framework to articulate what they're doing and why they're doing it.

For example, teaching a class on different types of prayer could be implemented alongside practice exercises of listening prayer, *lectio divina*, or meditation. After people have experienced these types of prayer, direct instruction provides a way for them to put the pieces together and understand it better.

Consider how Jesus used direct instruction in the Sermon on the Mount. That was teaching, pure and simple. Yet, for his disciples it was also in the context of their daily lives and experiences of living and traveling with Jesus.

Jesus also used direct instruction before the sending of the seventy-two: Do not take a purse; stay in just one house; eat what you are offered (Luke 10:1–12). These were among the preliminary instructions he gave them just before sending them out on mission. They received instruction, went out on mission, and then debriefed how that mission went after they returned.

Instead of lengthy classes, try doing direct instruction more like how Jesus sent out the seventy-two: Here are a few basics you need to know on the front end; now go out and try doing them, and then we can reconvene and talk about the experience. People don't need to know everything they will ever need to know at the very beginning, just enough to get started. Then they can learn more as they go. Sometimes direct instruction is simply a matter of putting words to concepts that people are experiencing.

IF YOU CARE ABOUT THE RESEARCH...
A NOTE FROM CHUCK

Direct instruction consists of a group of procedures in which teachers structure goal-oriented lessons. According to Barak Rosenshine, the instructor is in control of the goals, selects the material based on the learner's ability, and "paces the learning episode."[25]

A BRIEF RECAP

The proper use of each tool requires an understanding of the goals and process of discipleship. Like a skilled carpenter, we need to use the right tool for the job. We need to be open to the voice of the Holy Spirit as to what tool might be best to help us move people toward their goal of becoming more like Jesus.

As carpenter-apprentices, we can learn to use the right tools at the right time to shape each unique piece of wood for its unique, God-given purpose: "For we are God's handiwork, created in Christ Jesus to do good works, which God prepared in advance for us to do" (Ephesians 2:10).

The next couple of months were challenging for Rob as he struggled to find a way to teach his people how to disciple others. One day when he and Jim met, it was one of those gorgeous fall days when winter is just around the corner but you don't really believe it will ever arrive. They decided to go for a walk, their feet crunching in the leaves on the sidewalk.

"Tell me about it," prompted Jim.

One of the first challenges was helping people to see discipleship in the context of life instead of as a meeting. Some of the people flat-out refused the idea, considering it a watering-down of discipleship teachings. "Can you believe some of the people actually dropped out of the discipler training because of that?" exclaimed Rob in exasperation. "It's actually the opposite of watering down. But they're so focused on learning theology in the classroom that they can't see it!"

The other challenge Rob faced was trying to teach discipleship skills instead of discipleship content. There was so much more material on discipleship content, but he needed to teach people how to have real-life conversations: how to challenge and sharpen one another, question, and model skills. He quickly discovered that people found their favorite tools and used them for everything. "Not every situation requires a hammer, Burt. Try gradual shaping instead." "Caroline, sometimes you will need to confront. Not everything can be dealt with effectively through encouragement."

Getting people to step out of their comfort zones was long, hard, slow work, and sometimes Rob felt discouraged. "I am never going to get this right!" he sighed.

"I've always said it takes three tries to get something right—sometimes four or five," said Jim. "But Rob, you're headed in the right direction. I know that doesn't make it any easier, but hopefully it gives you a vision for the long haul. Because when this takes off, it'll go far. And you'll not only have disciples, you'll have disciples who disciple others—people living it out and teaching others at the same time. It's a powerful combination. It's like being a player and a coach at the same time."

"I'll try. But for today I'm at least glad for this last bit of autumn before winter. I'm going hiking with my snowshoeing friends today. That always helps me clear my head and have some fun."

CHAPTER 10

DISCIPLES ON MISSION TOGETHER

The next time they met, Jim walked into their coffee shop and saw Rob finishing a conversation with Stan. Through the windows, they could see snow blowing down the sidewalk, covering everything in a blanket of white.

"Jim!" Rob called out upon seeing him enter. "Do you remember Stan? He's one of our community group leaders who has also been a part of the discipleship triads. We've just been having the most fascinating discussion about the interplay between community and discipleship—individualism versus a more communal approach—and how we might be able to fit those together somehow."

"Yes," agreed Stan, "So fascinating that I'm late getting back to work! Great to meet you Jim, but I need to run."

As the door closed behind Stan, Jim asked, "So what's going on there?"

"Well, Stan is a long-time member of Alcoholics Anonymous," started Rob, settling back down into his chair. "He wouldn't mind me telling you that," he added, waving aside Jim's expression of objection. "Stan is very open about his involvement in AA. And today he was expressing concern about our discipleship approach maybe being a little too individualistic. He was telling me about some of AA's basic beliefs about community. In fact, that's one of the main reasons he was drawn to being a community group leader in our church. He really sees and experiences the value of a supportive network of people."

"I don't know much about AA," admitted Jim. "What was he suggesting?"

"More of an underlying philosophy than a specific practice, if that makes sense. As Stan described the way the AA community both supports and challenges one another at the same time, I was almost forcibly reminded of our conversation about Hebrews 10:23–25. We talked about that passage last winter, remember? That's what I really want our communities to look like, and—at least according to Stan—that's a lot of what the AA community looks like too."

When birds fly in a V formation, they are taking advantage of the updraft of air created by the preceding bird—essentially getting a free uplift of airflow. They each sense the airflow of the bird in front of them and adjust their position to take advantage of it. The result of this pattern is that the birds furthest back in the formation flap their wings less often, conserving their energy. Every so often, the birds switch positions; there's no constant leader. They rotate, giving each bird a chance to lead and a chance to rest a bit.

Christian community is like birds flying in formation. We, like birds, are communal creatures. Although sometimes you'll see one bird flying alone, they generally find it works much better to fly together as a group with other birds. This approach is especially necessary in times of migration. Like birds, we need each other more when we are embarking on a journey of discipleship—we need each other's support.

A supportive community is a group of people who gather regularly, considering how to spur one another on toward love and good deeds, encouraging one another. These are the people we gather together with to live out the one-anothers of Scripture, toward the end of all of us becoming better disciples. Each person takes responsibility for his or her own response to God, but community provides the environment within which that response is taken.

Our faith community provides the broader context in which disciplemaking takes place. No one person can represent Jesus fully to everyone. It takes a village: the Body of Christ. Jesus had all spiritual gifts; we don't. We need each other. Therefore, the broader faith community plays an important role in our discipleship.

THE TEMPLATE OF AA

Alcoholics Anonymous provides a great template for how we can support one another in community. Consider some of the following features of AA DNA:

Admitting we're not in control. Much as we would like to believe the opposite, none of us are actually in control of our lives. There are only two groups of people: those who admit they're not in control, and those who don't admit it. It's hard for anyone to acknowledge their lack of control over their life, but paradoxically, it can be especially hard for Christians. We often believe (falsely) that if we do the right thing, life will go smoothly. There is no scriptural basis for this heresy. Rather, we need to acknowledge our own powerlessness. The apostle Paul did:

> I do not understand what I do. For what I want to do I do not do, but what I hate I do ... For I have the desire to do what is good, but I cannot carry it out. For I do not do the good I want to do, but the evil I do not want to do— this I keep on doing (Romans 7:15, 18b-19).

Transparency. Transparency means honestly and openly admitting who we are and how we struggle. It's the opposite of hiding. It means not trying to look better than we are. Again, Christians in particular struggle with transparency because we labor under the false belief that we are supposed to be good— or at the very least, better than other people. Again, this is a heresy with no grounding in Scripture. Sometimes we even couch it in terms of presenting a good testimony: If others see the real me, they won't believe in Jesus. The reality is that no one else expects us to be perfect. If we try to present ourselves as if we *are* perfect, they'll know we're not being honest and we lose credibility.

Non-judgmental listening. In AA meetings, people listen, without crosstalk or interruption, to all manner of stories and behaviors that can seem irrational and even crazy on the surface of things. But they listen anyway, without interruption or correction, because they understand that there is power in having the space to talk, to hear oneself talk, to be heard and to be understood.

Willingness to say the hard things. Non-judgmental listening doesn't preclude the willingness to say hard things when it's truly necessary. AA people are not there to try to fix other people, but to share their strength, hope, and experience. In doing that, sometimes they need to say challenging things to one another—generally not in a group setting, but one-on-one with a sponsor. Done in that context and in the spirit of "I'm no better than you," such challenges can be heard as spurring one another on, rather than as judgment.

WHAT ABOUT THE CHURCH?

Consider what this kind of community could look like in the church. Imagine people who are honest about their own short-comings, but still willing to step into the mess of each other's lives. Imagine people who listen well without judging *and* without justifying. Imagine people who provide support and encouragement to one another, but who aren't afraid to challenge each other when necessary. As one new believer put it after attending his first house church meeting, "This is just like AA, except with Jesus in the center of the group."

How attractive would that be to others? This isn't a group any-one would accuse of pretense, judgmentalism, or lack of depth. This is what we as human beings want—what we are looking for.

This kind of community provides three types of support: emotion-al, instrumental, and informational. Let's look deeper into each of these areas to sift through what each type of support means and requires, and what it can look like in a faith community.

EMOTIONAL SUPPORT

Emotional support within a community of faith means an envi-ronment of love, empathy, trust, and caring. It means you have people encouraging you, praying for you, and cheering you on. These are the people who can laugh with you and cry with you, both in a way that helps you move forward in your faith.

Without emotional support, we have a sterile environment;
Christian community becomes nothing more than trying to
correct one another and fix problems. Instead, we need a holistic approach that includes compassion, empathy, and genuine bonding. When we have that, we have a community that
helps us move forward constructively. We have people who will
listen, instead of just trying to give us answers when we share
struggles. We have people who are alongside us on our journey.

It's within this kind of environment that people grow. Like a
plant needs water, air, sunlight, the right amount of warmth,
and nutrients in the ground in order to grow, people need holistic support—including the emotional component—to become
strong and healthy.

Since worship services in many churches are too large for people to know one another on a deep level, this type of support
most often falls to the small group. So what ramifications do
we see here for our small groups? It means that we need more
than just people speaking truth to us. Too often people just
give one another a Bible verse. Instead, we need to go one

level deeper, sharing strength, hope, and experiences with one another.

The point is not to fix someone else, but to be with them as they go on their journey. It's designed to be a non-threatening environment where people can be honest about what's really going on. That doesn't mean there is never confrontation and challenge—on the contrary. But it does mean that any confrontation is done from a foundation of love and respect. If people are not first loved and respected, they'll be running away.

> Love is patient, love is kind. It does not envy, it does not boast, it is not proud. It does not dishonor others, it is not self-seeking, it is not easily angered, it keeps no record of wrongs. Love does not delight in evil but rejoices with the truth. It always protects, always trusts, always hopes, always perseveres (1 Corinthians 13:4–7).

INSTRUMENTAL SUPPORT

Instrumental support refers to tangible aid and service. The early church practiced this kind of support:

> All the believers were together and had everything in common. They sold property and possessions to give to anyone who had need. Every day they continued to meet together in the temple courts. They broke bread in their homes and ate together with glad and sincere hearts (Acts 2:44-46).

This kind of support is very practical and down to earth. We're talking about coming alongside each other in times of financial need, giving parents of young children a night out, helping people move, giving food in times of sickness, texting a message of encouragement.

Remember that instrumental support is more than social work; it still falls under the umbrella of discipleship. We are providing instrumental, practical support to one another as we journey down the path of discipleship together. The relational component cannot be left out.

INFORMATIONAL SUPPORT

Informational support means guidance for handling problems. This type of support can take many different forms. It can be offered more formally in congregational settings: financial management seminars, parenting classes, informational seminars on various discipleship-related topics. It can take the form of resources like books, websites, or DVDs. Or it can be something as simple as a different perspective someone shares with you.

A community can find many different ways to come together, pooling information and resources to solve problems and share perspectives.

**IF YOU CARE ABOUT THE RESEARCH...
A NOTE FROM CHUCK**

Research scientist James House categorized four broad classes or types of social support: emotional, appraisal, instrumental, and informational. Based on his analysis of the extensive literature on the topic, he concluded that collectively these categories cover social support, while each category contains a number of specific acts. According to House's findings, social support plays an important role in reducing stress, protecting health, and enhancing the quality of our lives.[27]

THE VAST POTENTIAL OF COMMUNITY

When we come together as a Christian community in healthy ways, we become part of something greater than ourselves, and our collective potential for impact is vast. Not only is each individual supported, like the birds flying in formation, but together we receive clarity about the greater vision toward which we are all working. We can check each other's direction and cheer each other on.

We team together to make a difference, to be the hands, feet, and voice of Jesus in the world. We are serving individuals, but also making a difference in our schools and neighborhoods. We *are* good news—demonstrating it and sharing it at the same time.

Together we can keep one another on track toward this greater vision. Particularly when we partner with people with different gifts and strengths, we accomplish more and are able to see each other's blind spots. We can band together for support and stretch one another in our areas of weakness. Having each other around helps us maintain focus and keep moving forward toward the vision.

When we do that, our community is attractive to others and multiplies. As we encounter others, we discern and watch for those who are responsive and open, and invite them into conversation about what it means to be a follower of Jesus. If they can see how we are different, they will be able to decide if this kind of community is something they want to be a part of. In this way, new communities of Christ-followers grow and multiply.

TRANSFORMATION IN THE CONTEXT OF COMMUNITY

Above all, make sure your community is affirming that God is at work in people's lives. He is always speaking, urging us toward transformation and closer alignment with who he created us to be. We need to try to see people through his eyes. Cast the vision for the hope and change that is possible through the Holy Spirit: "With man this is impossible, but with God all things are possible" (Matthew 19:26).

Above all, affirm that God is at work in people's lives.

We need to remind each other of these truths. As birds travel together in a flock, we do better together. When one of us is tired, another can take the lead. We all need someone to encourage us onward sometimes, and all the more as we see the day approaching.

The heart of the change process for individuals is found in the context of community with others. Unfortunately, we have a contradictory tendency. We tend to be individualistic, while our faith is communal. We are to encourage, admonish, and teach one another: "Carry each other's burdens, and in this way you will fulfill the law of Christ" (Galatians 6:2).

Just as the life of faith is lived out in the real world among other people, growing in that faith is also best done in the real-life context of community—that means your family, your friendships, your ministry groups and teams, your coach or mentor, and those you are discipling and leading. Supportive community is critical to the growth and transformation process.

Rob spent some time that next week researching AA and other recovery groups. He was amazed at how well their idea of community fit in with authentic Christian community, and told Jim about it.

"It all lines up so well it's almost like it was planned that way! AA says you need to admit that you're powerless, that you can't make things right on your own, that you need other people, that you need to make amends, that you need to help other people to continue forward in your own growth. . . it's amazing. I need to start thinking through how to incorporate this into how we're approaching discipleship."

"That sounds like a good idea," agreed Jim. He looked out at the melting snow dripping off of the tree branches. "Given those similarities, it's really unfortunate how differently people view AA groups from church groups. Most people see AA groups as a safe place you can be honest about your shortcomings. And most people see church groups as a place where you have to pretend you have it all together and are better than you actually are. That's really sad."

Then they both sat in silence for a while, looking out through the glass wall of the coffee shop and sipping their coffee as it cooled.

CHAPTER 11

LIVING OUT THE GREAT COMMISSION

It was one of those rare pleasant winter days that makes you think that spring may be right around the corner. Usually it means there's still plenty of snow to come, but Rob and Jim figured they may as well enjoy the sun while it was out. They walked around the town on wet sidewalks, hearing the melting snow falling from the trees in clumps.

"You look happy this morning," observed Jim.

"You'll never believe what happened! Remember Burt, the older guy who's big into his antique car club? To be completely honest, he reminds me of the traditional 'grumpy old man,'" laughed Rob. "Anyway, Burt has actually brought two of what he calls his 'car buddies' to faith. I was stunned! I mean, this is a group of old guys, mostly retired, who usually do nothing but sit around talking about cars, tinkering with them, and trying to locate and trade spare parts. I did not see that coming!"

"Wow, that's great!" said Jim. "They may be old guys, but this ministry is already moving into the second generation. It's kind of like what we used to call the '2 Timothy 2:2 chain' when I was in Honduras. We lined up in order of who led who to faith and through discipleship. . . You know: Barnabas to Paul to Timothy to 'other reliable people.' At one point we had seven of us in one line. That was a day to remember.

"So," said Jim, shifting his attention to Rob, "What are you going to do to help Burt encourage these two new followers of Jesus to start sharing their faith with others? It's a multi-generational investment, and you want to be sure they keep passing it on. Usually these new followers of Jesus are far more open to sharing their faith than long-time followers."

"Yes, this is an opportunity," responded Rob. "And, in an unexpected way with the antique car club, it's kind of like seeing the gospel jump to the next village. This is Great Commission stuff!"

Last words are often lasting words. What are the last words Jesus said to his disciples?

> But you will receive power when the Holy Spirit comes on you; and you will be my witnesses in Jerusalem, and in all Judea and Samaria, and to the ends of the earth (Acts 1:8).

These words are why we've placed so much emphasis throughout this book on making disciples, not just being disciples. Jesus not only asked us to believe, but to follow him and to bear witness to the world around us. Being a disciple is active, not passive, and the reproduction of disciples is an essential part of that activity. Jesus told his disciples at the Last Supper, "Anyone who loves me will obey my teaching. My Father will love them, and we will come to them and make our home with them. Anyone who does not love me will not obey my teaching" (John 14:23–24).

Our obedience is the proof of our personal discipleship. If we love Jesus, we will obey his commands. What he did with us we will do with others. We are to seek to be the hands and feet of Jesus, serving and raising up others.

Serving God means reaching out to others and becoming part of the mission of Jesus. We take the freeing message of his gospel and reach out to our own Jerusalem, Judea, Samaria, and ends of the earth.

WHO ARE YOUR SAMARITANS?

Let's think about those places: Jerusalem, Judea, Samaria, the ends of the earth. They form concentric circles from wherever we are, from those closest to us to those farthest away from us.

It's usually easiest to love those in Jerusalem and Judea. These are our neighbors, the people who are like us in culture, values, language, etc. It's also relatively easy to love people at the ends of the earth. They're far away; we can send them things and feel good about it. We can go to visit for brief periods to help them. But the physical distance and their "otherness" keep them at a safe distance from us personally.

It's the Samaritans that present the real challenge to most of us—nearby, but different from us culturally. They may speak our language, but they don't usually share our values or perspective. We may not want our kids to play with their kids for fear of a "bad influence." We may not approve of their lifestyle. We may simply not like them.

It's our Samaritans who are the hardest to love. It's easier to love people across the ocean than those on the other side of the tracks. There's less history there. Consider yourself. Consider your church. Who are you neglecting? Who are your Samaritans?

There are still people who need to be reached and gathered around the throne in Revelation, people from every tongue tribe and nation—including our own. The kind of life Jesus has called us to is not just a self-centered me-and-God kind of existence. It is radically other-centered.

The kind of life Jesus has called us to is not just a self-centered me-and-God kind of existence. It is radically other-centered.

This kind of outwardly focused life means pushing on to the next place, the next town, the next village. It means having fresh expressions of the church crop up all over the place. What would it look like if the gospel of grace infiltrated every segment of society? What would it look like among the poor? Among the rich? Among those who don't speak our language?

Among the homeless? Among skateboarders? Among surfers? Imagine any subculture you want, set apart by language, economics, age, gender, interests, education. Every single one of those subcultures needs Jesus as badly as you do.

REACHING ACROSS THE TRACKS. . . AND ACROSS THE WORLD

So what will it look like for you and for your faith community to go across the tracks, both locally and globally? Bob's small house church provides an example. They reach their neighbors (Jerusalem and Judea) through relationship. They volunteer alongside some unbelievers who are culturally similar to them and share an interest in social justice.

The house church also serves globally (the ends of the earth) through giving to a holistic ministry in Madagascar focused on reforestation, employment, and a maternity home for single mothers. They identified a ministry where they—a small faith community—can make a meaningful difference across a great distance.

Finally, they serve in Samaria (those who are geographically nearby but culturally far different) by teaching anger management classes at the Salvation Army. Actually, they serve in groups of twos and threes in different ministries throughout their area: support groups for children, in-patient recovery homes, wherever people sense the Holy Spirit leading them. "All they asked was that we should continue to remember the poor, the very thing I had been eager to do all along" (Galatians 2:10).

None of us has to do everything, but all of us have to do something. Find out where people are gathering and meet them there. Listen for the voice of the Holy Spirit, and have the courage to step out in obedience when you hear it. That's how we carry out the Great Commission, and that's how the gospel jumps from village to village, and from country to country. Because we are always experiencing transformation ourselves, we will always have something to share with others. "We love because he first loved us" (1 John 4:19).

> *None of us has to do everything, but all of us have to do something.*

GENERATIVE DISCIPLEMAKING

Bob sometimes describes disciplemaking as "generative." Generative means you're not just discipling the person in front of you, but from day one you're discipling them to reach out to others, who reach out to others, who reach out to others. Therefore, we need to make sure we're discipling in such a way that what we're doing is readily reproducible. Barnabas discipled Paul who discipled Timothy, who discipled others (2 Timothy 2:2).

Discipleship is generative. As we grow, we make more disciples. As those disciples grow, they in turn make more disciples. The cycle becomes more fruitful as we go.

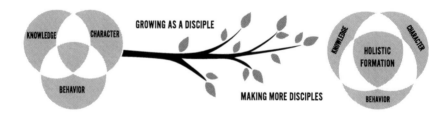

There is a great deal of power in the generative nature of discipleship. That's what moves us from making disciples by addition to making them by multiplication.

MULTIPLICATION

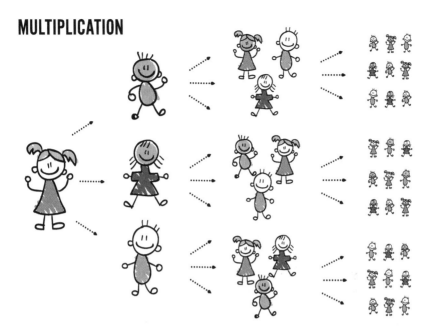

Becoming generative in our disciplemaking also ensures that we are taking a biblical approach to making disciples. Let's say we've made a disciple who does not make any more disciples. Is he truly a disciple when he is not living in line with the last commandment Jesus gave his disciples—to make more disciples?

Making disciples in a generative way has significant impact on church planting, for each person who comes to faith leads more to faith—and every person who comes to faith in this way understands that this is part of their mission. By focusing on discipling, you can actually see new faith communities emerge, multiply, and grow. Discipleship is the foundation that undergirds church planting and multiplication.

ON MISSION. . . TOGETHER

Discipleship is how we are called to seize the mission of Jesus. It extends far beyond how we live individually into how we live in community with others. We are to live corporately as the body of Christ in the world in a way that makes a difference.

The church has been specifically empowered for this purpose: After Jesus' resurrection, he instructed his disciples to wait in the city until they had been "clothed with power from on high"—by the Holy Spirit (Luke 24:49).

We can dig deep into what Jesus has asked us to do in the power of the Holy Spirit. With his strength, we—the church—can storm the gates of hell, and the gates of hell will not stand against us (Matthew 16:18). It will happen, but we need to do it Jesus' way. We need to put other things aside and focus on what really makes a difference.

Together as the body of Christ, we can reflect Jesus to the world around us by being the hands, feet, and voice of Jesus. That means raising up others, seeing new communities of Jesus-followers started, and becoming part of a movement that's much larger than ourselves—one that makes an outsized impact for the kingdom of God.

That's discipleship. It embraces both being a disciple and making disciples. In fact, when we look more deeply, the two are inseparable anyway. As we become more like Jesus, we reach out. As we reach out, we become more like Jesus.

> *As we become more like Jesus, we reach out. As we reach out, we become more like Jesus.*

So who can you start influencing? Who will you team with? When will you start? What rhythms will you put in place? That's the subject of our final chapter.

Next time Rob and Jim got together, the weather was good enough that they decided to go for a walk around the lake. They followed a hiking trail for a full mile around the perimeter of the lake as they talked.

"I'm not sure this whole multiplication thing is working, Jim," admitted Rob. "At least not as well as I had hoped it would. I tried telling Burt to get the new believers, Bill and Mac, to start thinking outward right away. But he doesn't really seem to understand how to do that. I'm concerned that this extension chain may be coming to a halt. It seemed like everything was going so well, too," said Rob with a frown.

Jim thought for a few minutes as they walked. "Remember how I say it takes three times to get something right? No one said this multiplication thing was easy."

"Certainly true," acknowledged Rob. "But I've been on this road with you long enough that I'm convinced it's worth it. Even if it takes more than three cuts to get it right," he added, with a smile.

MAKING A DIFFERENCE

You know what I'm noticing, Jim?" asked Rob. "It's something I noticed earlier, I suppose, but I keep seeing it crop up in new ways: Some disciples are just more fruitful than others. It's just like how some of the triads worked and some didn't, and how some of the people in them were willing to share their faith while others weren't. That story you told me about giving up on people who weren't fruitful didn't set well with me at the time. But I'm starting to see it not as giving up on some people, but about focusing on and investing in others."

"What does that look like for you?" asked Jim.

"I'm feeling more and more like I need to invest my time in some of the people who are more fruitful and really showing promise. Maybe I could start coaching them so that they know how to build in more reproducibility with those they're discipling."

"And who are those people?" asked Jim.

"Certainly Burt, who I mentioned last time. But I'm also thinking of Laurel, Stan, and Caroline. Caroline has been having some pretty intense spiritual conversations with people involved in the music school program where she teaches; that place could actually be ripe for revival. And Laurel has quite the group of teenage girls who have begun looking to her as a mentor. They are asking a lot of spiritual and ethical questions. Stan, our AA friend, has been growing his community group exponentially. He's really in the position of teaching others now.

"All four of them participated in that course I taught on discipleship tools—scaffolding, modeling, etc. I'd like to support them more as they learn how to use those tools more effectively," explained Rob.

If you want to see traction and growth in your discipleship endeavors, you need to start somewhere, even if your plan isn't perfect. We've laid out an approach to discipleship in this book, and we're sure it isn't perfect either. But ask yourself: "If not this, then what?" If you have a better plan, use it. If not, start with this one and refine it as you go.

The path of discipleship is paradoxical: You'll never be ready until you start. Don't try to wait until everything is perfectly laid out. It's easy to get stuck in theory: thinking about discipleship versus doing something about discipleship.

Only thinking, and not doing, is a recipe for getting nowhere. You have to start somewhere, even if it's not perfect. And the starting point is where you are right now.

What tools or processes do you have in place to comprehensively develop your people as disciples? Whatever you do, do something. And do it intentionally. To not respond with concrete actions is to actively decide not to make disciples.

> *To not respond with concrete actions is to actively decide not to make disciples.*

CONSIDER THE BENEFITS

Think through all the ways a healthy, intentional, clear process of discipleship could help your church or ministry. Discipleship spreads throughout the whole batch of yeast, lifting everything else along with it.

Increasing health. Turning the spotlight on discipleship, and helping people assess where they are and where they need to go, results in increased health across your congregation. You'll see stronger relationships, compassion shown to neighbors, outreach in the workplace. You'll see your people increasingly becoming the hands and feet and voice of Jesus, caring about the things God cares about, and putting kingdom priorities first. Imagine what you could do with that kind of congregation.

Measuring success in meaningful ways. Too often we measure success in our churches in the wrong ways: money and attendance. Take a step back and consider what success really looks like in the eyes of Jesus. The tree of discipleship helps us assess our congregations through the real-life, action-oriented lens of spiritual transformation. . . individuals, churches, and whole communities.

Helping you spot trends. As you shift the perspective from the assessment results of individuals to the broader pictures of your whole ministry or congregation, certain trends will come into focus. The data will speak for itself. While one size won't fit all, seeing a pattern of results will tell you something. For example, one or two areas of development might consistently be rated higher or lower than the others. In some cases, certain themes may even emerge as denomination-wide patterns. This type of data helps church leaders cooperate with what God's doing by addressing key issues in a more targeted, intentional way.

Creating a baseline for growth. Assessment results create a picture—a snapshot in time—of that individual. But the impact doesn't end there. Those same assessment results, when processed in the context of community, yield a direction for growth. By reflecting on them and being sensitive to the voice of the Spirit, a game plan for transformation emerges. Assessment results form a baseline of information that can be put to use. Taking stock of where you are helps you determine where you need to go. Future growth can then be compared to the original baseline.

Modifying your methodology, as needed. In light of the opportunity for formative assessment, any individual, group, or entire ministry can place greater or lesser emphasis on certain areas, depending on their stage of growth and the fruit of their efforts. Given that we all have a limited amount of time and energy, a balanced strategy is usually the best course of action. This should help us develop the holistic type of disciples we're aiming for.

Advancing God's kingdom through leadership development. A discipleship assessment releases the strengths of your people, maximizing the contribution they can make to advance the kingdom of God. There are resources in the body of Christ that we are responsible for stewarding well; developing disciples to their fullest potential is one way to manifest that good stewardship. When we understand more of who they are, then we can deploy them in ways that maximize their contribution.

PLANNING THE WAY FORWARD

You also know that doing what you've done in the past is going to get you the same results you've gotten so far. So what will you do differently?

There are a lot of different possibilities out there. The most important thing is getting started. Pick an approach and implement it. You can always make changes as you go. Gather with some others in your congregation and take some time to brainstorm in the following areas:

- Clarify what you're trying to produce with your discipleship efforts.
- Provide a reliable way for people to assess where they are in their discipleship process.
- Set forth a clear process for growth after the assessment.
- Help people measure where they're making progress.
- Figure out how to make discipleship reproducible in your context.

What are you trying to produce with your discipleship efforts?	How can people tell where they are in their discipleship process?
What is the process for growth after people have assessed where they are in their discipleship?	How can people measure where they're making progress?
How can you make discipleship reproducible in your context?	

TAKING THE FIRST STEPS

All congregations need a simple, flexible, yet focused system that can be replicated for making disciples at all levels. We need something that clarifies each of the five areas above. Creating a clear path forward for people to follow is essential for helping people get traction in their discipleship efforts. Here are a few additional questions to help flesh out a plan for doing that:

- Who are the people God wants you to invest in?
- How will you connect with them?
- How are you already engaging in the harvest?
- How will you model the way for others?
- Who are you going to be discipling?
- Who will you team with?
- How can you maintain an outward focus?
- How can you raise up others who raise up others?

Whatever you do, be intentional about discipleship. Don't just hope it happens by osmosis. Find someone to work with and help you stay on track. Then step back out of the way and watch what God does with your faithful work. Just see what he wants to do in and through you, for the sake of the world around you.

PUT YOUR HAND TO THE PLOW. . . AND DON'T LOOK BACK

When Bob was a junior in college at UCLA studying chemistry, he had a spiritual awakening. He became involved in campus ministry, a youth choir, and other activities. Life was very full, and Bob enjoyed the vast majority of what he was doing.

Before sitting down to study one day, this thought came into his head (which he now recognizes as God speaking to him): "Bob, why don't you sit down and figure out where all your time is going?" He thought that was an interesting question.

Besides, he didn't want to study anyway. So he calculated. His weeks were quite full with church, school, sports, relation- ships, etc. Then the prompt came to make a list of what Jesus had commanded us to do in Scripture. Bob did a side-by-side comparison between that list and how he was spending his time and the one command where he was doing nothing stood out to him: making disciples. And Bob recognized that it was a fairly significant command. It became very obvious to him that he needed to invest some time in making disciples. But his schedule was full. Where could he find the time he needed to invest? The only thing he could find that was flexible was the seven hours a week that he was spending in the youth choir. It became instantly obvious to Bob that he needed to quit the choir so he could make disciples.

There were two complications. One, the choir had a major performance in four weeks and he had a part in it. Two, he was dating the choir director's daughter at the time. Bob asked the Lord when he should make this change. In response, he found himself landing upon Scriptures such as, "No one who puts a hand to the plow and looks back is fit for service in the king- dom of God." So he made the decision not to delay.

First Bob told the girl he was dating, and then let her know that he'd talk with her father the choir director. No one under- stood his decision, including the senior pastor: "Why can't you just wait four weeks?" The youth choir was the social circle of the church, and Bob knew that his not being a part of it would eventually lead to the dissolution of the dating relationship he had; that was the core thing they had in common. Plus, there was nothing disciplemaking-related that was immediately in those time slots of choir rehearsals. He didn't yet know what he was supposed to do in order to make disciples. So why did Bob have to leave right away—especially when it made everyone angry with him?

Three days after Bob quit choir, the answer came. An oppor- tunity came through the youth pastor. The junior high youth group wanted to have a Bible study right before the evening service—directly during choir rehearsal. Bob would never have been tapped for that role had he already had a previous commitment. And he now had the answer for whom he needed to go and make disciples of—the junior high youth group. That decision launched Bob into middle-school ministry (and he still loves middle-schoolers) and into the general ministry direction his life has moved toward since then.

If you're already doing a lot and your schedule is full, God is likely not asking you to add one more thing. On the contrary, he may be asking you to drop something. Pray not only about what you're supposed to be doing, but about what you're not supposed to be doing. Whatever you hear, just be sure to respond in obedience, even if you can't see the full picture yet.

Through listening prayer, you may know the right thing to do, but it can be hard to actually do it. People may not understand. It might cost you, but it's worth it. Don't put your hand to the plow and then look back.

Quitting choir was the first step in Bob's journey of making disciples. What's your first step? What do you hear God calling you to do? What do you hear him calling *you* not to do? Who will you start with? Who will you team with?

There will be bumps along the way, but keep going. Keep moving toward transformation. Keep encouraging each other, keep learning from each other, keep sharpening each other... and all the more, as you see the day approaching.

"Hey, this is really working, Jim! Not everything, of course, but enough! I can really see my investment in Burt, Caroline, Laurel, and Stan flowing through them and into those they're discipling.

"Investment over the long haul is really what makes a difference," said Jim.

Rob continued, *"One of Laurel's girls asked about getting baptized. Instead of referring the girl to me, which I'm sure is what Laurel would have done in the past if this had happened, she felt confident talking with the girl about baptism and its meaning herself. And now this girl, Kira, wants to be baptized!*

"Stan has been mobilizing his community group to serve their neighborhood in some really practical ways, and the people in his group have begun establishing some relationships that way. They're going to have a community cookout next weekend, and have begun talking about starting an additional group. This new group will have more of the AA transparency and honesty. Should be an interesting experiment to see if we can replicate that DNA.

"Burt and Caroline have been hitting some walls, but there's still a lot of potential there. I'm trying my best to be a sounding board to help them think through the roadblocks they're running into.

"And you know what's really interesting? The people I've spent less time investing in haven't even seemed to notice. They weren't very invested in moving forward in their discipleship anyway, so it's like there's no net loss. Amazing!

"Now I'm feeling like I'm really focusing my energy where it needs to be focused. And I'm starting to see the transformation."

CHAPTER 12

CONTINUED?

Sunlight streamed through the windows and warmed their skin.

"I'm heading out of state in another few weeks to stay with my son and his kids for a while," said Jim. "I've been here near my daughter's family for a year and a half now, can you believe it? Now my son would like his fair share of free child care." Jim smiled. "I don't mind so much, actually."

"Well you sure have been here for me at a critical season," said Rob. "And you will be missed. Any idea what's next for you? I feel like this whole last eighteen months or so has been about me. I know you were wanting to spend this time trying to discern what God has for you next."

"I think I've been hearing from him pretty loud and clear actually. I may be technically retired, but God's not nearly done with me yet. And you helped me see that," smiled Jim, nodding at Rob. "I'm going to enroll in a coach training program. I think God may want to use me to help young ministry leaders like you—people with big dreams who are dissatisfied with the status quo. People with a fresh vision for a different kind of discipleship. Who knows?" he added, "I may even write a book someday."

"I'd buy the first copy," volunteered Rob. "You've helped me tremendously. Because of your investment in me, we're seeing new small community groups emerge that have a different DNA because they're being formed out of the harvest. We're seeing a dramatic increase in outward focus because of a new, more holistic understanding of discipleship. Fresh expressions of the church are developing through these promising leaders. And I personally am feeling so much more optimistic and energized by my ministry. I'm feeling better physically and made some new friends through my snowshoeing group too. We've decided to take up fishing in the summers," grinned Rob. "Mostly just as an excuse to keep hanging out."

Rob clasped Jim's hand. "Thank you for helping me move from 'thinking about it' to 'doing it.' I would never have gotten here if I'd tried to think my way through the whole thing beforehand. I'm grateful you encouraged me to just get started anyway, even if I didn't know entirely where I was going."

APPENDIX
Questions for Reflection, Discussion, and Action

Please use these questions together with your team, to reflect on the ideas presented in this book and to chart the course of discipleship for your ministry.

Chapter 1: Where's the Transformation?
- Where have you seen transformation in your personal discipleship journey?
- How have you experienced the dynamics between loving God, loving others, and making disciples in your life?
- What resonates with you about how Jesus made disciples? What challenges you?
- How have you adapted to the differences between individuals in your life and ministry?
- What's one step that you sense God wants you to take to move forward?

Chapter 2: What Does a Disciple Look Like?
- What qualities and behaviors are you seeking to develop in disciples?
- How does your description of a disciple compare to the tree of discipleship?
- What steps can you take with others to sharpen your picture of a growing disciple?
- Where are you progressing well as a disciple? What's next in your development as a disciple? Who can help you in that development?

Chapter 3: Discipleship Starts in the Harvest
- What experiences and individuals influenced you in the early stages of your spiritual journey?
- Describe your first encounters with Jesus. How did you respond?
- How are you personally engaging with people who don't yet know Jesus?
- In what ways are you encouraging the people you disciple to reach out to others?

- What promptings are you sensing from the Holy Spirit? What are the first steps you need to take, in response?

Chapter 4: Discerning What's Next in Your Discipleship Journey
- What are your current practices for assessing your progress as a disciple, and for determining what's next in your development?
- How do you incorporate feedback from significant others in your spiritual development process?
- How does God help you discern and confirm what's next in your discipleship journey?
- How can you help others assess their own progress in discipleship and to develop a personal growth plan?
- What next steps does God want you to take personally? In your ministry or church?

Chapter 5: The Mosaic Process of Discipleship
- How does your discipleship process reflect a mosaic approach? In what ways is it more linear?
- How has your own growth as a disciple been "mosaic"? How can remembering that help you to be flexible and intentional as you disciple others?
- In what ways can Scripture and other resources be integrated with a mosaic approach?
- How holistic is your development—hands, head, and heart? Which one needs more focus? In what ways?
- What can you do to facilitate the engagement of disciples with the mission of Jesus to make more disciples?

Chapter 6: Growing Together in Groups
- How do your groups live out each of the following discipleship dynamics of Hebrews 10:24–25?
  - Let us consider...
  - How we may spur one another on...
  - Toward love and good deeds...
  - Not giving up meeting together...
- What intentional and relational processes can you use to facilitate discipleship?
- Who do you know who is fruitful and faithful? How can

you and/or others invest in them?

- How can you help people take greater responsibility for their own discipleship growth?
- What next steps are you sensing God is asking you to take regarding community or groups?

Chapter 7: Dynamics of a Discipling Relationship
- How consistently are you connecting in your discipleship relationships? How could you become more intentional?
- What would you say your ratio is between affirmation and correction, as you develop others? How would the people you're investing in answer that question?
- What are some ways you could be more supportive of others in their discipleship journey?
- How can you help people focus their aspirations for growth into more specific goals?
- Which area(s) need more attention in your discipling relationships?
- What next steps will you take?
  - Intentional
  - Developmental
  - Supportive
  - Focused

Chapter 8: Obedience as the Crux of Discipleship
- What motivates you to respond to God in obedience? Why?
- When have you stepped out in faith to face your fears and/or take a risk?
- What helps you move into and through your discomfort zones? Why?
- How can you help your disciples face their fears and respond in loving obedience to the situations they face?
- What promptings are you currently sensing from the Holy Spirit? What will you do about them?

Chapter 9: The Tools for Making Disciples
- How do you disciple others in the context of life?
- What tools do you frequently use in your discipleship relationships?
    - Social modeling
    - Questioning
    - Scaffolding
    - Reframing
    - Shaping
    - Confrontation
    - Direct instruction
- Which tool(s) do you overuse? Why?
- Which one(s) do you want to sharpen or use more often? Why?
- What's your plan to grow as a disciplemaker? What will you do? How will you do it? When? Who will help you?

Chapter 10: Disciples on Mission Together
- How well do your groups provide an environment of love, empathy, trust, and caring that facilitates discipleship growth? What's your evidence for saying that?
- In what ways do your groups meet the practical needs of people? How could you become more effective?
- How do you help people come together to share information and resources to solve problems?
- In what ways are you teaming with others to serve and make a difference in the broader community and beyond? How could you increase your impact?
- What steps can you take to cultivate more and better supportive communities for growth and transformation?

Chapter 11: Living Out the Great Commission
- To what degree have you personally aligned your life with the mission of Jesus? How could you increase your outward focus?
    - In Jerusalem and Judea—those who are like you and local
    - In Samaria—those different from you who are nearby
    - To the ends of the earth—globally

- Who are the people or groups most difficult for you to love? Who do you unintentionally or deliberately avoid? Why?
- What promptings are you getting from the Holy Spirit as you look around you in listening prayer?
- How have you seen the generative process of making disciples in your life—making disciples who make disciples, who make disciples who make disciples?
- What next steps will *you* take to grow as a developer of reproducing disciplemakers?

Chapter 12: Making a Difference
- Respond to the following questions:
- What are you trying to produce with your discipleship efforts?
- How can people tell where they are in their discipleship process?
- What is the process for growth after people have assessed where they are in their discipleship?
- How can people measure where they're making progress?
- How can you make discipleship reproducible in your context?
- How could a healthy, intentional, clear process of discipleship help your church or ministry?
- Who shares your passion and vision for healthy discipleship that results in more and better followers of Jesus?
- How could you team with them to develop and implement a discipleship strategy?

About the Authors

Dr. Robert E. Logan has well over thirty years of ministry experience, including church planting, pastoring, consulting, coaching, and speaking. Bob has seen a great deal, yet remains on the cutting edge of ministry as he is currently planting an organic, missional network of churches in Los Angeles. Bob earned his DMin from Fuller Theological Seminary. Current favorite ministries include volunteering in a recovery community, and helping lead a house-church gathering.

Dr. Charles R. Ridley has utilized his expertise in the area of measurement and assessment in the development of the Church Planter Profile, which has shaped the foundation of church-planter selection all over the world. He has also done extensive work on coach competencies and assessments, conducting a qualitative international research project. A licensed psychologist and professor at Texas A & M University, Chuck earned his PhD in Counseling Psychology from the University of Minnesota.

ENDNOTES

Chapter 1

[1] Mark R. Lepper, Lee Ross, and Richard R. Lau, "Persistence of Inaccurate Beliefs about the Self: Perseverance Effects in the Classroom," *Journal of Personality and Social Psychology* 50 (1986): 482–491; David A. Levy, *Tools of Critical Thinking: Metathoughts for Psychology*, 2nd ed. (Long Grove, IL: Waveland Press, 2010).

Chapter 2

[2] Edwin A. Locke and Gary P. Lathan, "New Directions in Goal-Setting Theory," *Current Directions in Psychological Science* 15:5 (2006): 265–268.

[3] D. Louise Mebane and Charles R. Ridley, "The Role-Sending of Perfectionism: Overcoming Counterfeit Spirituality," *Journal of Psychology and Theology* 16:4 (1988): 332-339; David D. Burns, "The Perfectionist's Script for Self-Defeat," *Psychology Today* 14:6 (1980): 34–52; David Stoop, *Living with a Perfectionist* (Nashville: TN: Thomas Nelson, 1987).

Chapter 3

[4] Susan Goldin-Meadow and Sien L. Beilock, "Action's Influence on Thought: The Case of Gesture," *Perspectives on Psychological Science* 5:6 (2010): 664–674; Joenna Driemeyer, Janina Boyke, Christian Gaser, Christian Büchel, and Arne May, "Changes in Gray Matter Induced by Learning—Revisited," *PloS One* 3:7 (2008): e2669

[5] Paul G. Hiebert, noted missiologist and cultural anthropologist, proposed the theory of bounded set and centered set as a way of understanding social groupings: Paul G. Hiebert, *Anthropological Reflections on Missiological Issues* (Grand Rapids, MI: Baker, 1994); Other authors have popularized and applied his

ideas to ministry: Michael Frost and Alan Hirsch, *The Shaping of Things to Come: Mission for the 21st-Century Church* (Grand Rapids, MI: Baker, 2013); Daniel L. Guder and Lois Barrett eds., *Missional Church: A Vision for the Sending of the Church in North America* (Grand Rapids, MI: Eerdmans, 1998).

[6] Warren S. Brown and Brad D. Strawn, *The Physical Nature of Christian Life: Neuroscience, Psychology, and the Church* (New York, NY: Cambridge University Press, 2012).

[7] Lou Goble, ed, *The Blackwell Guide to Philosophical Logic* (Malden, MA: Wiley-Blackwell, 2001); Roy Moran, *Spent Matches: Igniting the Signal Fire for the Spiritually Dissatisfied* (Nashville, TN: Thomas Nelson, 2015).

Chapter 4

[8] The preeminent document on the standards of assessment has been jointly developed and endorsed by the American Educational Research Association (AERA), American Psychological Association (APA), and National Council on Measurement in Education (NCME). American Educational Research Association, American Psychological Association, and National Council on Measurement in Education, *Standards for Educational and Psychological Testing*, 2012 ed. (Washington, DC: American Educational Research Association, 2014).

[9] Three-hundred-sixty-degree assessment and feedback is used widely in the fields of human resources and industrial/organizational psychology. The technique has been shown to improve the performance of employees in the workplace. One major benefit is that it provides a correction to inaccurate self-perceptions that individuals have of themselves. Studies have shown that individuals tend to rate themselves significantly higher than other people rate them. Joy F. Hazucka, Sarah A. Hezlett, and Robert J. Schneeder, "The Impact of 360-degree Feedback on Management Skills Development," *Human Resource Management* 32:1–2 (1993): 325–351; Alan G. Walker and James W. Smither, "A Five-Year Study of Upward Feedback:

What Managers Do with Their Results Matters," *Personnel Psychology* 52:2 (1997): 393–423; Francis J. Yammarino and Leanne E. Atwater, "Understanding Self-Perception Accuracy: Implications for Human Resource Management," *Human Resource Management* 32:2–3 (1995): 231–235.

[10] Jennifer M. West, "Black Intelligence Test of Cultural Homogeneity," in Caroline S. Clauss-Ehlers, *Encyclopedia of Cross-cultural School Psychology, Volume 1, A-K* (New York: Springer, 2010): 164–165.

[11] Michael Scriven, "The Methodology of Evaluation," in Robert E. Stake, *Curriculum Evaluation*. Chicago: Rand McNally (1967). American Educational Research Association (monograph series on evaluation, no. 1).

Chapter 5

[12] Imitation plays a critical role, not only in the development of children, but in the formation of adults. The process is continual and affects our motives, goals, attitudes, and behaviors. The apostle Paul articulates his imitation of Christ in 1 Corinthians 11:1: "Follow my example as I follow the example of Christ." His comment includes the twofold function of making disciples while becoming a better disciple. See also chapters 4–5 in Warren S. Brown and Brad D. Strawn, *The Physical Nature of Christian Life: Neuroscience, Psychology, and the Church* (New York: Cambridge University Press, 2012).

Chapter 6

[13] Charles R. Ridley and Steven J. Goodwin, *Confronting Dysfunction* (St. Charles, IL: ChurchSmart Resources, 2010).

Chapter 7

[14] Raymond G. Miltenberger, *Behavior Modification: Principles and Procedures*, 5th ed. (Belmont, CA: Thompson, 2012).

[15] Used courtesy of Dennis Easter, Foursquare Pastor.

Chapter 8

[16] In the United States, approximately fifteen percent of individuals experience an anxiety disorder sometime during their lives. In the mental field of psychology, a distinction is often made between fear and anxiety. Fear is considered an emotional dread or terror of something specific, like an object or event. Anxiety is considered an emotional discomfort that is not directed to a specific object or event. The feeling is more vague and diffuse. However, the distinction is not always clear-cut because dread due to identifiable and unidentifiable objects and events can coexist in a person's experience. Robert J. Sternberg, *Psychology: In Search of the Human Mind* (Orlando, FL: Harcourt Brace, 2001).

[17] There are two primary ways of exposing people to the sources of their fears and anxiety. On the one hand, *flooding* as in intervention entails immediate and hard-hitting exposure such as the above example of exposing the dog-phobic person or putting a child who is afraid of drowning immediately back into the water. On the other hand, *systematic desensitization* entails gradually exposing the individual to the noxious stimulus, such as helping a child who is afraid of puppies by using a combination of relaxing the child and slowly moving a puppy closer from a far distance to the child while playing. In both strategies of exposure, the keys are that the individuals experience no harm from the noxious stimulus, and they are not allowed to escape the situation (Miltenberger, *Behavior Modification*).

[18] Dietrich Bonhoffer, *The Cost of Discipleship* (New York: Macmillan, 1966).

Chapter 9

[19] Albert Bandura, *Social Learning Theory* (Englewood Cliffs, NJ: Prentice-Hall, 1977).

[20] Paul D. Eggen and Don P. Kauchak, *Educational Psychology: Windows on Classrooms*, 8th ed. (New York: Merrill, 2012).

[21] Lev S. Vygotsky, *Mind in Society: The Development of Higher Psychological Processes,* Michael Cole, Vera John-Steiner, Sylvia Scribner, & Ellen Souberman, eds./trans. (Cambridge, MA: Harvard University Press, 1978).

[22] As a technique used in counseling and psychotherapy, reframing owes its origins to two well-known psychotherapists. In the 1950s, psychologist Albert Ellis began to focus on changing what he deemed as clients' profound self-defeating beliefs. In the 1960s, psychiatrist Aaron Beck began to focus on changing what he deemed as clients' cognitive distortions—their systematic errors in reasoning. With both psychotherapists, the goal is to replace clients' destructive thinking with more constructive thinking—in the case of Ellis, rational beliefs and in the case of Beck, the way people process information. Aaron T. Beck, A. John Rush, Brian F. Shaw, and Gary Emery, *Cognitive Therapy of Depression* (New York: Guilford Press, 1979); Albert Ellis and Robert A. Harper, *A Guide to Rational Living* (North Hollywood, CA: Wilshire Books, 1997); Thomas L. Sexton, *Functional Family Therapy in Clinical Practice: An Evidence-Based Treatment Model for Working with Troubled Adolescents* (New York: Routledge, 2011).

[23] The technical term for shaping is the differential reinforcement of successive approximations. The differential reinforcement part means that a specific behavior is reinforced in a particular situation, while no other behaviors are reinforced. The successive approximations part means that reinforcement begins with a *starting behavior,* stops when new a behavior occurs that more closely approximates the desired behavior, and then reinforcement resumes with this new, typically is more complex behavior. The process of starting, stopping, and restarting of reinforcement continues until the target behavior is eventually reached. Burrhus F. Skinner, *The Behavior of Organisms: An Experimental Analysis* (New York: Appleton-Century-Crofts, 1938); Miltenberger, *Behavior Modification: Principles and Procedures,* 4th ed. (Belmont, CA: Thompson, 2008).

[24] Confrontation is a micro-skill designed for use in counseling

and psychotherapy, although it has much broader application in improving human functioning. Charles R. Ridley and Steven J. Goodwin applied the skill to leaders in ministry. These authors explained the two phases of confrontation. In the first phase, critical examination, the purpose is to determine whether the behavior in question is a problem and needs to change. In the second phase, direct challenge, the purpose is to connect the problem behavior to its causes and consequences in order to help the person change. Charles R. Ridley and Steven J.Goodwin, *Confronting Dysfunction*.

[25] Barak Rosenshine, "Content, Time, and Direct Instruction," in *Research on Teaching: Concepts, Findings, and Implications*, Penelope L. Peterson & Herbert J. Walberg, eds. (Berkeley, CA: McCutchan, 1979), 38.

Chapter 10

[26] Carl R. Rogers. *A Way of* Being, (New York: Houghton Mifflin, 1980); David E. Orlinsky, Michael H. Ronnestad, and Ulrike Willutzki, "Fifty Years of Psychotherapeutic Research: Continuity and Change," in *Handbook of Psychotherapy and Behavior Change,* 5th ed., Michael J. Lambert, ed. (New York: Wiley, 2004).

[27] James S. House, *Work Stress and Social Support* (Reading, MA: Addison-Wesley, 1981).

Made in the USA
San Bernardino, CA
12 February 2019